SO-AIK-070

**ALSO BY JIM MORRIS**

*War Story*

**AVAILABLE FROM
ST. MARTIN'S PAPERBACKS**

# FIGHTING MEN

## JIM MORRIS

St. Martin's Paperbacks

*To my stepfather, William Merrill Morris,*
*who taught me what it is to be*
*a man in this world*

Published by arrangement with Dell Publishing.

FIGHTING MEN

Copyright © 1993 by Jim Morris.

Cover photograph of Green Beret and map © Photri.

ISBN: 0-312-98484-7

Printed in the United States of America

Dell Books edition / April 1993
St. Martin's Paperbacks edition / May 2003

St. Martin's Paperbacks are published by St. Martin's Press, 175 Fifth Avenue, New York, NY 10010.

10  9  8  7  6  5  4  3  2  1

# CONTENTS

## WARRIORS

## JUMPERS

## POW/MIA

## VETERANS

# FOREWORD

Late in his life, I became a friend of James Kern Feibleman, Professor Emeritus of Philosophy at Tulane University, and described by Huntington Hartford as "the greatest mind of our era." The explanation for this friendship was simple; he had outlived all his friends and peers, who ranged from Robert Sherwood to Albert Einstein to Alfred Knopf to Gertrude Stein, and had need of a companion who shared his interest in good food, great cognac, and watching the Thoroughbreds run.

If a friendship can be said to be a partnership, I got the best of the deal. We both understood from the beginning that I was not an intellectual, and that whatever he had to say to me was going to be phrased with that in mind, in other words, simply. He didn't seem to mind, for he was first and foremost a teacher. Now that he's gone I realize that the only real education I ever received was—sometimes literally—sitting at his feet.

I had just begun to write about—and thus think about—the profession of arms and its practitioners, and our conversations often turned to the subject of war and warriors.

"Considering how recently we climbed down from the trees," Feibleman told me, "I am surprised at how few wars we have, not at how many."

I asked him where warriors came from, and his response was that they traced their ancestry back to the men who left the fire in the cave and went out to battle with the saber-toothed tiger, and with other men who coveted their fire, their food, or their women.

If those who went out to do battle came back victorious, they quite naturally presumed they were entitled to the closest place to the fire, the most appetizing piece of roasting meat, and their choice of the women.

"We humans invariably get in trouble," Feibleman told me, "when we try to pretend we are not animals."

Exactly as one dog in a pack dominates the others, so did the warriors dominate their tribe. The females didn't mind, for being the warrior's female meant they would share the spot close to the fire, the best food, and have their young protected.

The nonwarriors, like lesser male lions snarling and baring their teeth—but not quite brave enough to do anything else—while waiting for the pride-leader to take his full of the kill, spent their time plotting the downfall of the dominant—warrior—male.

Feiblman made me understand that the warrior class exists today. Interestingly, he felt the police should be classified as warriors, something that doesn't seem odd if one thinks of the solitary policeman patrolling alone in the narrow streets of North Philadelphia or the South Bronx.

There is no doubt that the finest warriors of this century have been the Americans who fought their wars outside the restrictions of conventional military organizations. In the Second World War these were the Marine Raiders, Merrill's Marauders, and the OSS Teams we dropped into occupied Europe. In Korea they were the Irregulars on the East Coast and Task Force Able on the West—now officially recognized as predecessor organizations of Special Forces. The exploits of the Green Berets (and those of their brothers in the SEALs, Marine Corps Recon, and Air Commandos) in Vietnam, Laos, and Cambodia need no recounting here.

But I would like to offer this observation: I was in Las Vegas with Jim Morris early this year, at the Special Operations Association Reunion. SOA is open to anyone, sailor, Marine, airman, or soldier who did combat in some sort of special operation. The man who commanded the First Special Operations Group in World War II was there, and so was a Green Beret colonel who had to leave to (we later found out) prepare to go to Panama.

There was gray hair, but their backs were still straight and the eyes were bright with intelligence. Most of them had done remarkably well in civilian life, proving that Feibleman was right again, warriors do get the spot closest to the fire, the best piece of roasted meat, and the most desirable women.

Major Jim Morris was medically retired for wounds suffered during his three tours as a Green Beret in Vietnam. His credentials as a warrior are beyond question. It has been said that it is impossible to vicariously experience what went on over there, but *Fighting Men*, it seems to me, gives the reader the privilege of doing just that.

—W. E. B. GRIFFIN

# INTRODUCTION

These stories are about soldiering, and the aftermath of soldiering. They are about warriorship, the kind where you risk your life in combat, and the kind where you risk your life in life. They are about my friends and me and what we did and what has happened to us, and about what that means if it means anything at all.

They are about my friend Larry Dring, who was, among other things, the best small-unit leader I ever knew, and about Chuck Allen and Project Delta, which was the finest combat unit I ever fought with. Delta was the prototype for all the Special Forces reconnaissance units in Vietnam, and for the division LRRP units, and for the SOG Command and Control operations. The SOG units, particularly CCN, have become more famous in the aftermath of the war, because their missions were more highly classified, and because their casualty rate was higher, but I believe Delta was a more professional unit, simply because it had more control over its own operations.

That's an arguable point, and my experience with SOG is even more limited than my experience with Delta. When you're operating way over the edge like that, those kinds of distinctions are negligible anyway.

Maybe it's not possible to tell how it was, even though I intend to try. I had read *From Here to Eternity* eight times and *Catch*-22 six before going into combat, and all they did was whet my appetite. Young men are crazy.

# FIGHTING MEN

# WARRIORS

# Ranger in Paradise

Larry Dring is one of those odd kinds of friends you make in the military, because you're always moving around and people phase in and out of your life. Before writing his story I had seen him only a dozen or so times, but there was always a good feeling between us and I had been able to keep track of him over the years through the Special Forces old-boy network.

We met in 1962 after I fractured my coccyx on a night jump in Korea. Larry picked me up off the drop zone and took me to the hospital.

I was hurting, but not so much that I couldn't stop for a cup of coffee with him. I was then a first lieutenant and he a staff sergeant. He was fairly short, but strongly built, and wryly funny, an adventurous spirit. In the army they usually call that being a wiseass.

Not content to let me star with my brand-new jump story, he told a wild tale of having been the minister of agriculture of the Republic of Korea for a brief period during the coup that installed Chung Hee Park.

Later, at the hospital, I was given a chemical heating pad and a bottle of Darvon. "That's it?" I asked the doctor, a fat captain who was unhappy at being awakened at 0300.

"Contrary to popular opinion, young man," he replied, "we cannot put your ass in a sling."

I didn't see Dring much over the next few years. We were both in the 1st Special Forces Group on Okinawa, but in Group we played leapfrog in and out of Vietnam on six-month temporary-duty (TDY) tours. With Vietnam and our other commitments, it was not unusual to be in the same company with a man for two or three years and never meet him.

But there were stories about Dring. Once, on Oki, I saw him driving his jeep down Highway One: He had bought it as salvage from quartermaster sales, and painted it solid black with military-style bumper markings. The left one said DING and the right one said DONG.

Rumor was that he had ripped off a new engine for it from a shipment at the Da Nang Air Base, painted the box it came in OD, stenciled his Okinawa address on it, then run it over on a forklift to the regular weekly Marine C-130 for Kadena Air Base on Okinawa and sent it to himself. It was waiting for him when he went home.

Later I heard he had gone to Officers' Candidate School, which was difficult to believe. A big part of OCS is spit and polish; I'd never seen him in a completely correct uniform, and didn't know anyone who had. Maybe it wasn't Larry; not many people knew him by his first name.

The Dring under discussion was a legendary Mike Force commander. The Mike Force—Mobile Strike Force—was an airborne reaction force battalion maintained by Special Forces in each of the four Corps Tactical Zones of Vietnam, with another at the Group headquarters in Nha Trang. Led by American Special Forces advisors, their soldiers were what we were forbidden to call "native troops." In the Central Highlands, where this Dring's company operated, the "indigenous personnel" were Montagnards, most of whom belonged to FULRO (Front Uni de Lutte des Races Opprimées: United Front for the Struggle of the Oppressed

Races), the Montagnard revolutionary organization, eager to fight any Vietnamese, who fought on against the new regime for ten years after the fall.

This legendary Lieutenant Dring had gone home only a month before I returned in the summer of 1967; if he was Larry I had missed him again. But the following spring my Larry Dring sauntered into our embarrassingly plush officers' club at the headquarters of the 5th Special Forces Group, where I was then the Information Officer. We were both captains. As usual, he was rolling—laughing, telling loony stories that always checked out.

"Some jerk captain down in Saigon tried to send me to the 9th Division. I told him 'Hey, in case you don't know it, sweetheart, there's a new reg' "—which Dring made up on the spot—" '460-12, that says if you get three Purple Hearts and volunteer to come back to Vietnam you can pick your unit. Well, I got five Purple Hearts, and if I don't go to Special Forces I'm getting back on that airplane and goin' back to the Land of the Big PX.' "

So they sent him to Nha Trang, where our adjutant, a man not noted for the flexibility of his thinking, wanted to send him to the Delta.

"Oh, no," said Dring. "I'm going to the 24th Mike Force Company. We've been corresponding. We've got operations planned."

"I'm the adjutant here," replied our adjutant, an officious, piglike major. "I make the personnel assignments."

"Well," replied Dring, "you can cut orders for anywhere you want, but tomorrow morning I'm gettin' on a chopper to Pleiku, to the 24th Mike Force Company. If you want me and the orders to coincide, that's what you'll cut orders for."

Two months later I was at lunch in the club when Dring walked in again. I hailed him over to show off to some of my staff-officer buddies. Most of us had been around awhile; we had all been on "A" detachments in combat, either as captains or lieutenants. Fairly often we went on hairy expeditions of our own, so we were not easily impressed by the standard animal act. But he impressed them.

"What are you doing here?" I asked him. "I thought you never came out of the woods."

He sat down and ordered lunch. "Got some grenade fragments in my back a couple of weeks ago and forgot about 'em," he said. The others at the table raised their eyebrows a little. "They festered, so I had to come in and get them fixed. Look at this. They sewed 'em up with wire."

We looked and sure enough they had—but what impressed the staff officers was the fact that he was wearing bloodstained NVA underwear and an NVA belt. He explained that the American advisers in his company went on thirty-day operations in NVA country—Blackjack Operations—without a belt on their trousers. Walking ten to twenty klicks a day in hundred-degree heat, eating just what they carried on their backs, they lost so much weight on those patrols that they had to kill somebody and steal his belt in the first two weeks or their pants fell off.

He started kidding me about Psychological Operations, which had been one of my staff responsibilities when I'd been stationed at Pleiku. "I'll show you Psy Ops. We got nineteen in one ambush on this last operation—big infiltration route, everything but a yellow line down the middle and stop and go lights—and buried them beside the trail with their right arms sticking out with a note in each hand that read, *Surrender or die*. That's Psy Ops."

Despite his reputation for ferocity in the field I never knew Dring to drink, smoke, curse except under extreme duress, or carouse with women. He spent his free time scrounging rice and clothing for missionaries to give to refugees. The missionaries' kids called him "Uncle Larry."

That meeting was the last time I saw Dring in the Army. I heard later that he had been badly wounded in downtown Pleiku during Tet '68, been cared for by a missionary nurse, and married the girl. But before I could follow up on the story I was wounded myself.

A year or so later I was a graduate student at the University of Oklahoma, having coffee at a table with a group of students, all of whom were at least two of the following: disabled, veterans, or writing students; I was the only one who was all three, although my disability was not particularly significant except that it put me out of the army.

One of the ex-GI writing students was an Englishman named Rick Rescorla. Rescorla had been successively a sergeant in 22SAS on Cyprus, a London bobby, a commando officer in Northern Rhodesia—now Zambia—and a reconnaissance platoon leader in the 1st Cavalry Division in Vietnam. When we met he was a student, an English major, and concurrently a member of the Oklahoma National Guard, Senior Tactical Officer of the 45th Division's Officer Candidate School. When I couldn't top his stories with my own I started telling Dring's.

It turned out he and Dring had been OCS classmates.

I asked him, "How did Dring get through OCS?" I had no doubts about his abilities, but I couldn't visualize him in a highly polished helmet liner and spit-shined combat boots. According to Rescorla, Dring spent most of his time in OCS wearing a French camouflage jacket and red beret, giving weapons demonstrations to ROTC cadets.

In 1973, working as a correspondent in Thailand, Vietnam, and Cambodia, I went to Lop Buri, then headquarters of the U.S. 46th Special Forces Company. Lieutenant Colonel Bill Radtke, the commander, said I had just missed Dring. He was still a captain, still had his leg in a dropfoot brace—and was still making parachute jumps on it—and his job assignment was Psy Ops. But Psy Ops was a cover for him, as it had been for me in a way, and he did his Psy Ops over the border in his old accustomed way.

All the preceding stories about Dring were included in my book *War Story*, and when it came out Dring wrote me.

I wanted to see him again, and eager to do it at someone else's expense, convinced Bob Brown of *Soldier of Fortune* magazine to hire me to write an article on the legendary Mike Force commander.

I scanned the Charleston airport trying to find a familiar face; I hadn't seen him in twelve years. What would he look like?

A Huck Finn–like ten-year-old kid in a khaki jumpsuit with a name tag that read LARRY approached me. He wore U.S. parachute wings and a fatigue cap.

"Your name Dring, kid?" I asked. He pointed to the corner where Larry Dring stood, leaning on a cane, leg in a brace, wearing khaki pants, a Cambodian army field jacket adorned with Cambodian parachutist wings, and an Afrika Korps cap with a Combat Infantryman's Badge and U.S. master blaster wings on it. Same old Larry. He still wasn't in the right uniform.

Dring drove us to his home. We caught up on the way. He said he was working on an advanced degree at a local university, not the Citadel, a civilian college. After completing that he planned to make a career out of helping Asian refugee children adapt to American society, a process he'd had to go through himself after twenty years in the army, about half of it in the Far East and the other half in the mountains of north Georgia as a Ranger instructor. During the next two days neither of us could stop talking.

# Ranger Dring

Larry didn't wait until he was a Mike Force commander to become a legend in his own time. He was too prone to get caught up in arguments, coups, and revolutions for that. We talked about his adventures as a young sergeant and I asked him how old he had been when he joined the Army.

Dring said, "I was two days short of seventeen. I put in a year in the Guard until I was old enough to go in the Army.

"I had a friend, Henry Miller, who'd been in the Army Air Corps in WWII. He was a hustler, and he showed me the ropes. When I went on active duty with another friend, we showed up with three pairs of faded, slick-sleeved, tailored fatigues and spit-shined boots. Anybody can spot issue stuff. We stowed that in the footlocker. The cadre figured we were reenlistees and made us platoon leaders, and the mess sergeant told us to go flake out in the storeroom while everybody else went to KP. It wasn't hard, after military school, marchin' those guys. Gettin' over like a fat rat at seventeen.

"I went in the 504 Parachute Infantry Regiment. I was a bugler in military school. I can't read music . . . strictly by ear. Before they found out I could play the bugle I was in the pits. One day they were lookin' around for somebody to play the bugle and I just happened to be sittin' in the head shed. The bugle was there and I was playin' with the mouthpiece. The sergeant major asked me if I could play.

"I said, 'Yessir.' That afternoon I was a PFC.

"Each battalion had a bugler, by TO&E [Table of Organization and Equipment]. I played for four or five months, and I was gettin' ready to be regimental bugler and a corporal. Oh, boy, that's a small unit god, with two hard stripes. I auditioned for the job and got it.

"But they had a reorganization and dropped the slot and I got replaced by a record player. There went my two stripes.

"I was lucky. I was in the 82nd Airborne Division and when I was nineteen I went to Ranger School. Before that they put me in the signal platoon."

I asked him if he made buck sergeant when he graduated from Ranger School.

Dring replied, "I was supposed to, but makin' E-5 was contingent on three things: Did you get the Ranger tab?" —the Ranger School customarily dropped thirty to sixty percent of a class, and even if you finished you might not be awarded the Ranger insignia, probably the most coveted personal decoration in the peacetime army—"Did your tactical officer recommend you? Did the parent unit concur?

"That was usually a foregone conclusion. But they'd put me in the signal platoon and sent me to signal school. I didn't want to go but they went by IQ. In airborne units at that time you wore a size-three hat and a size-forty shirt. They had a commitment"—an order to send someone to signal school—"and they figured, 'Well, he's got an IQ, we'll send him.'

"So I came back with a ciphers and teletypes MOS, Military Occupational Specialty. I was really locked into Signal, but I didn't want any part of it. I wanted to go to Ranger School, but every time a commitment came down for Rangers, some sergeant or lieutenant would get it. My chances as an E-4 were those of a snowball in a furnace.

"The reconnaissance platoon sergeant told me, 'I'll get you in recon if you go to Ranger or Pathfinder school right now.' One night I was sittin' in the head shed on CQ—Charge of Quarters. I started readin' the regulations. I found I could apply for a service-school quota rather than directly to Ranger School. In other words, I could apply to the division headquarters so that the next one that came down would have my name on it. A month later there were four commitments—and Dring. So I went to Ranger School. But I was still an E-4 when I came back; my parent unit didn't concur, because I'd made so many waves to get out of the signal platoon.

"I could have made sergeant, and it wouldn't have cost them a thing. But they got the word down at Ranger School: 'The parent unit said no. He's young and immature.' The school got frosted, because they'd just about cut the orders. It created a little ill will.

"I was back at the unit one week when they decided to put E-4's on KP. Being a D, I was one of the first ones. Okay. Breakfast: A couple of comics came through the line. 'Ho, ho ho! You gotta be a Ranger to go on KP?'

" 'Now we're gettin' Ranger-qualified KPs.' Ho ho ho for breakfast. By lunchtime it was old. Enough!

"Suppertime, here came the clown, a real sarcastic comedian, administration platoon no less. He started that same baloney—and that was it.

"I reached across the serving line and grabbed the dude with one hand. I dragged him across the chow line, bopping him in the face all the way. His boots went in the meat and potatoes. That put the skids on supper for the hundred guys in the line. They pulled me off the guy, who was a little bent out of shape with one boot full of potatoes and the other full of meat.

"The cook was really indignant about this, because he'd have to cook up some hot dogs right quick—and the company commander just happened to be there. He was acting company commander, a first lieutenant. He was in the Signal Corps, but he was a mustang out of Korea. He'd won a Combat Infantry Badge as an enlisted man, came up through the ranks.

"I was called to his office; I had to wait outside. First the cook went in and told his story; then the other guy went in and told his. They both sat there smirking when I was called in.

"The lieutenant said, 'What have you got to say for yourself?'

"I said, 'Sir, I know you're gonna take my stripes, and that's all right. My only request is I want to go to a rifle company.'

"He looked at me and asked, 'Why?'

"I said, 'Sir, I want to go to a rifle company and be a soldier.'

"He said, 'Don't you think you're a soldier now?'

" 'No, sir.'

" 'What platoon are you in?' he asked.

" 'Sir, I'm in the signal platoon.'

"He was wearing his ODs with big signal brass and he had a Silver Star and a Purple Heart; he was no slacker. But I stood looking him right in the eye.

"He looked right back and said, "I'm a signal officer. Don't you think I'm a soldier?'

" 'No, sir,' I told him. 'You're a signal communicator.'

"He came up from behind that desk and I backed off, but he just stood there and said, 'Were you going to hit me, corporal?'

"I knew it: Lock City! 'Sir, I thought you were gonna hit me.'

"He said, 'If you didn't leave the headquarters company where would you want to go?'

"I said, 'Sir, I'd like to be in the reconnaissance platoon.'

"So instead of busting me and putting me in jail he transferred me to recon. That's where I made sergeant. A year or so later I joined the 77th SF Group and became a medic."

# The Minister of Agriculture

After training with the 77th, Dring's first assignment was as a medic in the 1st Special Forces Group, on a team that rotated between Korea and Okinawa. The team advised the Korean Special Forces—during which time Larry studied the history, customs, and language of Korea.

"I learned a long time ago to back off and see what the Indians were doing. For instance, when I was a corpsman in Korea it snowed a lot and we used to operate at night. I'd have to carry an M5 aid kit—and it got heavy.

"One day a Korean guy came in. He had the clap and I squared him away, filled him up with penicillin.

"He asked me, 'How much do I owe you?'

At the time I couldn't speak Korean. I could speak Japanese, though, and he had a little English.

"I got the message across. 'You don't owe me anything, pal. This is what I do for a livin'.'

"He was ecstatic. In his army it would cost him. So he sat down with me in this little Korean house. We got some straw and he taught me how to wet-weave strips of it. I thought, *This is very nice; I'm makin' little doilies outta grass, killin' time.* I felt like Rumpelstiltskin. I had some five-thousand-pound-test suspension line in my pack so I didn't really need the straw.

"But I thought, *Back off. Find out what he's doin'*.

"At that time the Army had slick shoes. In winter when we walked, we walked in leather. When we stood still we took the rubber bunny boots off. Actually most of the time in Group we'd just chuck the heavy-monster thermal boots because they made prunes outa your feet. You just had to make sure you kept your feet dry.

"So this Korean guy took two pieces of weavin' about ten feet long, and I noticed a lot of the other Koreans had 'em. There were only two Americans, me and Jimmy Gabriel." Gabriel was later the first American Special Forces man killed in Vietnam, for whom the Gabriel Demonstration Area at Fort Bragg was named. Dring was best man at his wedding.

"I thought, *What do I need this weavin' for? I need it like leprosy*. But I tied it on my pack. Nighttime came along. Blip. Time to go.

"The Korean said, 'Wait! Wait!' I wanted to make sure that I got in motion. I had my little stick and my carbine—and I wanted to make sure I could wobble.

"The guy started wrapping the weavings around my feet. I thought, *What in the world? What do I need this wrapped around my feet for?*

"We started up that hill and old Gabriel had a world of hurt because he was slipping, since our boots had slick bottoms on their feet. Me, I just swooped right up that hill. Those straw things were traction devices for your feet.

"If you can't learn something from somebody else, shame on you."

Dring made good friends in Korea, and the best was a captain named Kim. When Dring was transferred to Okinawa he took most of his leaves in Korea as Kim's houseguest. Korean custom dictates that houseguests attend parties to which the host is invited. At one of these parties Dring made what was to prove an important acquaintance.

Dring explained, "I met General Chou Moon Huan before the coup, at a party. I was sittin' in the last seat down. Nobody knew me. Somebody wanted to send a servant out for something, and somebody else took out a couple of coins. One of them, about the size of a quarter, had a picture on it of a turtle boat, a little boat covered with shields.

"The Japanese navy came into Pusan Harbor to X out the Koreans in 1500, but the Koreans had what was in fact the first ironclad ship. They Xed out the Japanese navy and that kept Japan off their backs for a couple of hundred years. 'Course the Japanese never forgot it.

"But the coin plopped out. I wasn't lookin' at my friend but at this other guy with the coin. Kim was almost on ice because I was there—but he'd had to bring me and he was kind of hoping I'd disappear into the upholstery.

"I walked over to the man and said a few words to him. It was a new coin. I said, 'Oh, that's the turtle-boat coin.'

"He said, 'Oh, yes.'

"Everything got quiet. When the main mug talks in Korea everybody else shuts up. He said, 'How do you know about the turtle boat?'

"Poor Kim almost went under the table because the general was talking to me, a sergeant, and he knew if I said the wrong thing, it would put him under the ground. And I knew it, too, because that's how it is in the Orient.

"I said, 'I believe, sir, that it was the boat of Admiral Ne Son Shi in Pusan Harbor in 1500, when he defeated the Japanese.'

" 'That was 1515,' he said.

" 'Oh boy. Excuse me.'

" 'How did you know about the turtle boat?'

"Everybody else—a couple of carloads of Korean colonels—just shut up.

"I said, 'Well, sir, I studied Korean history, and it's very interesting that it was the first time an ironclad had been used and it defeated the Japanese navy.'

" 'Come here!'

"I didn't know if he was going to shoot me or what. I went up there and he made me push some colonel out of the way.

"He said, 'You speak Korean?' So I said something in Korean.

" 'Very good accent.'

"I said, 'I'm trying, sir, but I still have to improve my vocabulary.' I was still on ice, wondering if I was sayin' the right thing. If I said something wrong, me and my friend were both gonna be in a bag.

"He said, 'What else do you know?'

"I said, 'Well, sir, I've studied your country.'

"Of course, he'd had a few snorts at the time. He said sarcastically, 'We have many advisers who come to tell us many things, but they don't read about our country.'

"I said, 'You have a very interesting history, sir.'

"We batted a few things back and forth. I knew some of the main points. It was like knowing who George Washington was. Then he wanted to know how I got there. I didn't know what to say. I almost bit my tongue on that one. How would he take a sergeant being a good friend of a captain?

"He said, 'You should come to more parties.'

"It warped his torque that I didn't drink. He wasn't bombed, but he was happy. He looked me right dead in the eye and asked, 'Do you smoke?'

" 'No, sir.'

"Oh, you must be a Christian.'

" 'Yes, sir.' And he thought that was neat."

In the spring of 1961 Dring went back to Korea, because he wanted to get his Korean parachutist wings. That's a big thing in the airborne, to jump with a foreign army, and usually the host nation awards their parachutist wings to be worn over the right breast pocket. Those wings were an especially big deal in the days before Vietnam, because it was hard to win a flashy decoration in the peacetime army.

Foreign wings were about the best status symbol a young soldier could hope for. Colonel Robert W. Garrett, who commanded the 1st Group when Dring and I were in it there, wore a different pair for every day of the week.

The Koreans didn't pass them out like cocktail peanuts, though. They required five jumps to qualify, and Larry had made four.

Dring and a friend on the resident U.S. team which advised Korean Special Forces hooked up with what they thought was going to be a mass parachute drop with a field exercise after. They borrowed a Korean jeep, put on Korean camouflage fatigues, and joined the convoy.

The convoy did not go to the airbase, however. It joined another group and headed out to the presidential palace to take over the country. After their convoy ran several roadblocks and threw a platoon of Korean MPs over a bridge, the two young American sergeants cut out of the column and went to the headquarters of the Korean Military Assistance Advisory Group to report what was going on.

The colonels and the general who advised Korean units went into a nut roll as the two sergeants identified the units that had been participating in the coup. They demanded to know how Dring knew what units were involved.

Dring told me he said, " 'Well, the artillery units had M42 dusters and Quad 50's, and the Eighth Division was wearing Eighth Division patches.' It really didn't require a Sherlock Holmes to figure it out."

"The colonel said, 'How do you know?'

" 'Because we were there with 'em.'

"They asked how we knew about the ROK Airborne Brigade.

" 'Well, their boss is leadin' 'em.'

" 'How do you know?'

" 'Well, I saw the guy's name on a list. I know him. His name is Chou Moon Huan.'

"The colonel started playin' games with me. 'How do you understand these things?'

" 'Because I speak Korean.'

" 'What organization are you with?'

" 'First Special Forces Group.'

" 'What?'

" 'Okinawa.' I was from Okinawa. The other guy was from Kimpo. They went bughouse.

"They sent us out to drive downtown and do some snoopin', find out what was going on and report back.

"We were the only Americans out. It turned into a real bummer, because the first day they didn't censor the newspapers, which said the Korean Special Forces came down and held a police call, with American advisers."

I asked him if that meant him.

Dring answered, "It wasn't us. They saw a couple of guys on pass walkin' around. Of course, we were still wearing Korean army uniforms. It was the only thing we had to wear, though we could have gone out in our underwear, I guess.

"We went downtown and met a couple of Koreans, one of whom we knew. I asked him if he could help me find my friend, Captain Kim. He couldn't help us. We finally bumped into Kim on the street. We gave him back the jeep. The Koreans needed the vehicles and it relieved us of the responsibility. This left us on foot.

"Kim said, 'C'mon along for the ride. I'll take you.' We went down to the Bando Hotel. In walked a sergeant, and he had an unhappy-looking Korean in a business suit next to him. Kim was playin' with the sergeant's grease gun, checkin' it out. It was an M3 submachine gun.

"I asked the sergeant, in Korean, 'Who's that guy?'

"Old Kim looked up and said, 'Oh, he's the minister of agriculture.' He put the grease gun on the guy and asked me, 'Would you like to be the minister of agriculture?'

"So that's what they called me around Group for a while, the minister of agriculture.

"We finally got back to Group about one o'clock. By this time things had changed. The newspaper reports had come out about the American advisers, so they wanted us to stay in the background. It wasn't us, but after that nobody wanted any part of us.

"Some other things happened. General Magruder was the commander of the Eighth Army and the United Nations forces, so he was ostensibly commander of the ROK army. He said, 'Order those insurgents back to their camps.'

"Well, c'mon; this was a coup. The Koreans in it had their necks on the block. It was either go for broke or find another country. Then the ambassador came up and ran his mouth, saying he wouldn't deal with anybody but the old government. By this time, however, there wasn't any old government.

"Chung Hee Park was the new main man. So the general and the ambassador had to be relieved. They'd ruined themselves with the new regime. Nobody would obey them and they were on their way out.

"But before this happened, we were sent over to Magruder's office in Eighth Army Headquarters. The general said, 'Who are you?'

"We were still wearing Korean uniforms and by now needing a shave. We looked grungy.

"I said, 'Sergeant Dring, 1st Special Forces Group, Okinawa.'

"He said, 'First Special Forces. I didn't know we had Special Forces over here, Sergeant.'

" 'I'm from Okinawa, sir.'

" 'What are you doing up here?'

" 'I'm on leave.'

"I was the only cargo on the next C-130 on its way back to Okinawa. I didn't even get a chance to go to Kimpo to pick up my bags.

"They put my friend on the next available slow boat goin' home. You ever hear of a guy gettin' thrown out of Korea?

"When I requested leave, I had gone to old Pappy Leechford, C Company sergeant major, a real nice guy. He said, 'I dunno, Dring, if I should approve this leave. Every time you go someplace it rains. No matter where you go something happens.'

"Before getting on the plane to go back to Okinawa, I told the radio operator—we had direct contact, and it was very informal—'Hey, just put a little message on there, to C Company; say, "Pappy, I didn't do it.—Dring." '

"When the coup started, the 1st Special Forces Group commander, Colonel Robert Mills, wanted to see all traffic coming out of Korea. The first thing over his desk was, *Pappy, I didn't do it.—Dring*.

" 'What is this? Who is this?'

"So they called Sergeant Major Leechford: 'Why is Dring in Korea?'

" 'He's got a lot of friends in Korea.'

"And then the airplane came in with just me on it, and they got the message, 'Pick this dude up.' I was still wearin' a Korean uniform and, by this time—it was almost a day and a half now—I was beginning to smell ripe. I went to see the colonel. All I had with me was a wallet, my passport, and a handful of Korean MPC [Military Pay Currency] that I didn't have a chance to cash in.

"The colonel asked me, 'Did you know about the coup in advance?'

" 'No, sir, I'm just a sergeant.' I was getting scared—getting thrown out of the country by a four-star general, and now they wanted to know what I knew. They were asking me, 'What did you have to do with it?' 'I didn't have anything to do with it.' I really didn't, but nobody would believe it.

" 'What about the message?'

" 'I just sent it as a joke.'

"By this time the coup had blown over, and everybody in Korea thought it was funny. But on Okinawa nobody thought it was funny. They wanted to know why I was there, why I had a Korean uniform, why I had a passport—and how come I was in the middle of it.

"I told them I was going to jump. 'I want to get my wings.' I got 'em. A Korean general whipped 'em on me. I had only four jumps but he gave 'em to me anyway.

"About six months later a SEATO"—Southeast Asia Treaty Organization—"Special Forces conference was held on Okinawa. They had people comin' in from New Zealand, Taiwan, the Philippines—and Korea. They needed people with a Top Secret clearance to drive staff cars, and they got mostly Special Forces people, including me. I drove out and stood in line. Somebody got off a plane and the first driver got him.

"I stood there waitin' and Colonel Mills was waitin' for a delegate—the one from Korea, General Chou Moon Huan. The colonel was standing a little to the side when the general walked down the ramp. He got ready to walk over to him.

"But the general walked over to me and said, 'Ahh, Dring! How are you?' And the colonel gave me this who-is-this look.

"Everything had blown over, and here was this Korean general officer just off the airplane. 'I have something for you.' He didn't say what it was.

"I got it about three days later. It was a book of poetry he had written and privately printed."

# Dring's First Patrol

I had always wondered how Dring could be so kind and considerate in garrison and still have a reputation for unbridled ferocity in the field, but he told me a story that answered my question. It was not a jolly lark like the Korean coup story. It was an incident that changed Dring.

In 1962 he was on his first patrol in Vietnam. His team had been assigned to Camp Plei Do Lim. The countryside there has been described as being like the terrain around Fort Benning—pleasant, with mountains, but not high mountains; forested, but not densely forested. The Montagnards of the area, the Bahnar, are a gentle, friendly people. It's the sort of place where you'd like to go on a picnic.

Dring's guide was an SFC named Frank Quinn. Quinn was a dried-up little guy with about twenty-seven Montagnard bracelets on his right arm, who chain-smoked overhand. He had been a prisoner of the VC early in the war; they had repatriated him with the warning that if he ever returned to Vietnam they would make a point of looking him up and killing him. He had three tours after that.

On the first day out they went into a Bahnar village, and Dring held a sick call. He treated everybody there, including one old man with emphysema—gave him a shot of epinephrine, which would help for the couple of days before the patrol returned.

They made a five-day loop of the area and came back in through the first village to do a follow-up sick call. They discovered the VC had executed every man, woman, and child there for "collaborating" with the Americans by letting Dring treat their illnesses.

Quinn put out a local security patrol and Dring was left to organize the strike force into a burial detail. Dring was sick to his soul. It was, I believe, the low point of his life.

Before all the bodies were buried, the local security patrol came back with a VC they had found on a hilltop with a PRC/6 radio.

"He was a real comedian," said Dring.

The VC, a barefoot young Vietnamese, wore tailored OD fatigues. He had a smirk on his face. He singsonged something in Vietnamese.

"What'd he say?" Dring demanded.

The interpreter told him that the kid had said, "You better be nice to me. The ARVN will let me go, and I might meet you in these woods again."

It was true. At that time the Vietnamese would turn loose Vietnamese VC who were captured by Montagnards.

Dring picked up a Browning Automatic Rifle and emptied a full magazine into him. When the strike force pulled him off he was holding the BAR by the barrel and trying to smash the corpse into a pulp with it.

When he tried to treat one of his own troops a few minutes later, he found that his hands were burned almost to the bone by the smoking barrel of the BAR.

That incident conditioned Dring's attitude toward Vietnam. "I didn't think this was right, and I didn't think it ought to happen anymore," he said.

Dring spent most of the next five years trying to make sure that it didn't.

# Indigenous Personnel

Larry gained his greatest fame in Vietnam as a Mike Force company commander. Not only was he the finest small-unit leader I have ever known, but he had a unique ability to get along with his Montagnard troops. He was amused by American notions of superiority.

"I'll tell you one about 'superiority' that I think you might get a bang out of," Dring said. "I and my company were out with the 1st Cav, Bong Son. The Americans were headin' up this big valley. It was back in about '67.

"There were little fingers coming into the valley and the Americans were goin' straight up. There was about a mile difference between us. I was ridin' the ridgeline. I was supposed to be flank security. I had about a hundred to a hundred fifty guys. The Americans had a battalion, and I had a company.

"This'll bring joy to your heart. You remember Pok time—from eleven or eleven-thirty A.M. to about two, when it got too hot and you knocked off. We always figured if the Americans wanted to do their stuff, we'd catch up; we walked faster than they did anyway.

"We were buzzin' along about ten-thirty when we bumped into big bunches of blackberries—all over the place. So we stopped to eat them. What's the difference:

ten-thirty, eleven-thirty? I sent out security and told them, 'I'll rotate and you can come back and get your share of blackberries.' In fact some of my guys brought 'em along for supper, there were that many.

"We plunked down at the head of a little draw; if we'd walked for another hour, we'd have been five klicks out of there. I heard gunfire. I got a pair of glasses and I looked down in the valley. Along came an American bunch pushin' about twenty VC up the draw. I got on the radio. I figured, *Hey, man, we'll just horseshoe this thing.* I finally got the message through that we were sitting at the top of the draw.

"So we horseshoed it, and some of the guys were still eatin' blackberries. We just sat there, and when Charlie came up we caught 'em. Twenty of 'em: *Bang, bang, bang, bang.* None of 'em walked out of that valley. We Xed 'em out and the battalion CO was ecstatic.

"Finally the Americans came up, and—hey, wonderful thing—they were telling everybody how they did this good deed. My people were the ones who really hosed Charlie down, because we just let 'em walk right up the barrel, and Xed 'em out. We had really good fire discipline.

"So we hosed the VC down, and the Americans were overjoyed. They policed up the brass and they brought the bodies and the guns out and all that stuff. They were really superheroes. It was a nickel-and-dime operation; that was about the only contact we had during the week and a half to two weeks we were out.

"Came back in later and one of the guys told me that the battalion commander of that outfit got the Legion of Merit for planning this intricate hammer-and-anvil operation. The company commander got a Silver Star.

"And the only reason we were there was because of a blackberry bush."

# Tips

"I learned something from a German SFC when I was in Ranger School, a lesson I never forgot. He'd been in World War Twice and he fought Americans. Other Germans you talk to fought Russians. Well, this guy fought Americans. You asked him and he told you.

"He was there with a German captain, an artillery-man, fantastically good with maps, and a fruitcake lieutenant, a little punk kid. They were comin' through to learn something about our Ranger School so they could start a German equivalent. They called it the school of the airborne individual fighter. You know, in German the name comes out eight feet long. They're just like the Chinese—they keep on addin'.

"We went out on a fire-and-maneuver exercise at night. M1 rifle, cartridge belt, and a couple of bandoliers. *Bangety-bangety-bang.* Next morning we came in and we had to turn in unused ammo, clean our weapons, and go to chow. The sergeant was in front of me. Most of the guys just turned in two to four clips. He got up, took one bandolier off, then he took another one off. Then he open up his pouches—nine clips.

"I turned in my four or five clips and I walked over to

him and said, 'Hey, Ray! Didn't you fire your weapon last night?'

"He looked at me like I was a nut. He said, 'Ja, ja, I fired.'

" 'Well, you didn't fire very much. How many times did you fire?'

"He looked at me and saw I was serious. 'I fired three times.'

" 'Everybody else was shootin' all night. Why did you only fire three times?'

"He looked at me like I was stupid and held up three fingers 'I only saw three men.' No doubt in my mind what would have happened to those three guys. I used to beat that into my people's heads when I was a company commander in Vietnam.

"In my company they only fired if they were being shot at—and if they weren't being shot at it was gonna cost them. They lit a cigarette in the field after dark, it'd cost 'em. They made a lot of noise, it'd cost 'em.

"We did not make a lot of noise, but when we fired somebody'd roll over and die. Most Americans would shoot at people. Just see somebody and start shootin' at him. Most people on automatic only make noise.

"Look, when they're runnin' around, if you start shootin' too soon you're gonna lose 'em. If a guy's walkin' away from you, let him go. If he's comin' across your front, wait until he gets directly in front of you. Then if you miss, you can shoot again. When a guy's comin' at you, just stand there and watch him. He'll come right up to the muzzle. If he wants to throw his hands up, great. If he doesn't . . . remove his head.

"That's why I used to have an M1A1 carbine and a thirty-round magazine. 'Course I only put about twenty-seven rounds in it, or on the short fifteen-rounders, about twelve rounds. All tracer. And I'd alternate lead-round magazines with tracer at the bottom, so I'd know, *I'm out of ammunition; it's time to change.*

"I had the solid tracer because I was the company commander. I wasn't gonna shoot anybody. I was gonna direct traffic. If I decided we needed to shoot anybody I'd jump up and start goin' *bang . . . bang* on semiautomatic. My men would see me. They'd see the tracer. If I shot, where would they shoot? On the tracer. Where were the bad guys? On my tracer. Some commanders just want to run around with a gun and make noise. That's not the purpose of the exercise.

"The most deadly weapon you have is the handset of your radio: Keep cool and call in air strikes. By the way, tracer is good for air-ground. Tell the pilot, 'Fire on my tracer.' "

# Splash

Both Dring and I had great admiration for one American commander, Colonel Francis J. Kelley. Kelley, a former New York City cop, was a staff officer with the OSS (Office of Strategic Services) in WWII. He looked a little like Raymond Burr and was, I think, the smartest man I met in the Army.

He earned his nickname, Splash, due to a fondness for water jumps; he did not want to splatter his corpulent, middle-aged body all over a hard drop zone. Kelley came to Special Forces from the Pentagon, went to jump school just before coming to Okinawa, and broke his leg on the second jump. They gave him the wings anyway, which did not endear him to a unit that was sixty-percent master parachutists. That didn't bother Kelley, and he didn't hesitate to run the Group as he wanted to. After Okinawa he commanded the 5th in Vietnam.

Kelley had majors and colonels running scared—but he liked Dring.

"Kelley's a funny guy," Dring told me. "Old Irish policeman. If you were on the right side of him, you had it made—but you'd better be right.

"I was down at Lung Tan and we were bein' shelled. I was the only officer—a second lieutenant. A camp was being put in there, and our Mike Force company was watching the store while the camp was being built. It was in the middle of no place, and Charlie had come in on it.

"WHAM! We returned fire with the four-deuce"—a big mortar—"until I noticed fire coming out of the bottom of the mortar. I said, 'Whoa! Cease and desist. That's it, pal.' But the 81's didn't go out far enough. Charlie was being cool. We didn't broadcast the fact that we were out of four-deuce to him, but the sitreps that I sent in said, 'Hey, we really are in a bag, because Charles is gonna come in on us without a four-deuce.'

"When the four-deuce went out it really got serious. The Cong started to come a little closer, and we couldn't keep them out. They couldn't get at us, because the 81's would still do them a job, but there was a little town next to us, and they did a number on it. Dependents lived there.

"It was a murky night with a slow drizzle. Plenty of flares. We had a few people Xed out but the horror that was done to that village. The VC came in and they knocked the livin'—they shelled the life out of it, and there was nothing our people could do.

"Charlie figured they'd get the dependents, not us. They didn't have a hole to get into or anything. And all we could do was fire the 81's. We could only get about a thousand meters out from the town. With a sixty millimeter they could hit the town and we couldn't hit them. With the four-deuce we could have done 'em a job.

"Because I was a medic, had a medical background, I used to monitor equipment. We were treating the indigenous people, and all we had left was a couple of M5 kits. I had been putting my requests in marked 'Emergency.'

"So now I got on the radio, and I started. Man. I got unhappy. I got on the voice single-sideband. I got some guy on the other end—I didn't know who he was and didn't care. I told him in no uncertain terms what I thought of him.

"He said, 'What's going on?'

" 'Whattaya mean, what's going on, you sorry—Don't you people read sitreps? The last twenty days I've been sending these things in 'Emergency.' Don't you idiots read? Don't you ever get off your dead butts and go to the S-3 and read? These people down here are out of medical supplies. And they're out of four-deuce. If we'd had the four-deuce in the first place it wouldn't have happened. You sorry people up there?'

"Splash put another couple of people on, and I told 'em what I thought of them. I said, 'You people go and read your sitreps and you'll find out what the problem is.' I told 'em the VC were hitting us from the other side of the local village and if we'd had the four-deuce we could have stopped them.

"I said, 'We're in a bag. We're tearing sheets up for bandages.' We didn't even have compresses. Man, I was hot. Absolutely empty, and requests, itemized and explaining why, right down the line, going in.

"That night Splash went and looked up those sitreps: They started Routine; then we needed a little more; then it got serious and then it went Emergency. The paragraphs got fatter and fatter. And Splash went back and put his S-4 on the first airplane and sent him out to us. He didn't just tell him; he put him on the plane—and Splash was on the first plane out the following morning.

"When we heard the planes were coming in, we had to put out gas pots in a square on our landing strip. It was a thousand-foot dirt strip—and the rain really put the skids on it. The later it got the muckier the runway got. And every now and then some little guy with a sixty millimeter mortar was sayin', 'Whoo-hoo, we're still here.' Three aircrews got air medals that night, and they earned them. Particularly the last pilot in.

"We had five litters and forty-two litter cases. We were putting them on in ponchos. The five litters had two people per—we were throwing them on. Instead of one four-deuce they sent us four. We didn't have crews for them. We had the ammunition but we didn't have crews. All we had was one team.

"Like I say, with Splash, if you're right, you're right. He came out the next morning and saw the place. We had earned our money that night. I showed Splash the four-deuce. It had a hole about the size of a dime in the base of it. I don't know how long the hole had been there. I don't know how much longer it would have gone before blowing us all up. You could almost miss the hole. It was a zigzag but you could put a medical probe through it.

"I showed Splash and he got the message about how many people we'd sent in. We only sent litter cases. We had walking wounded all over the place. You know how it is in a battle. We were in the process of cleaning up.

"We had a gun that fired a hundred rounds and there were canisters all around. That's a lot of ammunition. I used to teach my men to keep a couple of five-gallon water cans in the mortar pit. If somebody says you can only shoot so many rounds per minute, that's baloney. You take the water cans and start pourin' water not in it but on it. And you cool it down.

"They talk about minimum range; I'll give you minimum range. Take all those increments off and jack it up. Put out a couple of ammo boxes and stand that thing on end. Even with a four-deuce I've done it. I've had rounds wobble up, and some of 'em didn't even get to nose down. They came down sideways and didn't go off. Tell me about minimum range.

"When Splash came out there were still a couple of 81 rounds layin' out sideways. He was a sketch. I was telling him the story and he didn't say a word about it being him on the radio. The poor S-4 officer was looking for a hole to climb into. He didn't want to be around.

"Finally, Splash asked, 'Was that you on the radio last night?'

"I said, 'Yessir!'

" 'Kinda disconcerted, weren't you?'

"I didn't want to say too much, because I didn't want to use the ugly words. But I was still hot. I said 'Whattaya gonna do to me? Shoot me? Send me to Vietnam? Whattaya gonna do—have a look at this?'

"He said, 'You know you were kinda brisk out there.'

" 'You know how it is, sir,' I said. 'Sometimes you run into dummies.'

" 'I was on the radio. You were talking to me.' He thought it was funny. He never said another word about it."

# Christ Jesus

"You run around and do your thing and then you ponder later.

"I'd gone a month without bread. Rice twice a day is not bad, but I wanted to eat some bread, and we were five kilometers from some Americans. So I took a squad and whizzed on over.

"I was talking to the company commander in a clearing. Just us two. 'Course he had on his iron hat and his flak jacket and all that, and I was in my tiger stripes.

"Y'know, people abuse the word *sniper*. I used to ask the question: 'If you saw three guys in a clearing and one had a radio, who would you shoot at? Everybody answered, 'The guy with the radio.'

" 'No, you shoot the guy next to him. He's the guy you want, not some PFC. You want to shoot the platoon leader.' A sniper knows that kind of stuff. He usually picks on somebody that looks different.

"Well, I was standin' there rappin' with this guy. And a young kid, about seventeen or eighteen, walked right in front of me. Just happened to be walking by. And one shot rang out.

"*Bango!* Just one shot. The kid had a steel pot on. Got it canted. The round caught him right under its lip. Hit the helmet, spun back, and killed him. Dropped him and he fell right in my arms. I was standing there talking and I just put my arms up.

"The kid did it inadvertently, but Christ Jesus would have done the same thing for me with both eyes open. And here's something else—it was Thanksgiving. How do you give thanks? Do you say, 'Thank you, Lord, I'm alive and he's dead?' It's a soul-crusher. I appreciated being alive but I wanted that little dude to be alive too."

# Splish-Splash

"I had to deal with Kelley one other time. This is a long story—so hang on.

"I had a Mike Force company at Song Mau, and I was going to pick up a payroll. I missed the airplane. Saturday afternoon, I was sittin' by the runway on my rucksack in a camouflage suit, scratchin' my head; no rank insignia on or anything like that. I was a captain then.

"I didn't know what to do. The next scheduled run was Monday. Some dude walked up in a khaki shirt, khaki pants, and a leather belt. I thought he was a bulldozer operator from one of the civilian companies. He came up and looked at me and said, 'Howth the war goin', tiger?' I believe he had false teeth; his jaw was going from side to side.

"I thought, *What a banana*, and I said 'Well, it's the only war we got.'

"He said, 'Well, keep up the good work, tiger,' and walked away.

"*Who the devil was that?* I thought. *Is he mentally maladjusted or something?*

"Then a little Air Force guy came out: 'Did you see Robert Mitchum?'

" 'Who?' And then it dawned on me. Yeah, that was

Robert Mitchum, going around, inspiring the troops—by wriggling his jaws.

"While I was sitting there, gettin' over that one, along came another guy in khakis, uniform looked like he ironed it with a hot rake. He walked over and he had some brass that I'd never seen—crossed leaves. He was a Seabee or Navy engineer or something.

"He stopped and looked at me, and I thought, *What is this, a Halloween party?*

"I said, 'What are you?'

" 'I'm the Navy, champ.'

" 'Whose navy?'

"He said, 'I'm in the junk force.'

" 'What's the junk force?' I asked.

"He sat down and told me. He had a little boat and a Vietnamese crew and they drove up and down the coast and looked for smugglers and suspicious boats.

" 'You wanta come with me?' he asked. He added that every now and then he got into a little firefight. 'What do you know about a sixty-millimeter mortar?'

"I looked at him. 'What do I know? I invented it. Whattaya mean, what do I know?'

"He told me that every time his boat went by one spot it drew fire from the beach. The beach was flat as a pancake for a couple of hundred yards, maybe fifty feet of sand dunes and then you got the Sahara Desert. He said when the shooting started he'd get in close and shoot back. He'd get on the radio, because he had a friend who was captain of a little minesweeper in the U.S. Navy and it had a forty-millimeter on the front. The junk boat would go in and play target. Then he'd call his friend with the minesweeper and it would go in and *bang, bang, bang* into the beach.

"He asked me to come look at his boat and meet his crew. It was a little wooden boat like an oversized rowboat and its gunnels were ten inches high. Outstanding. There was a little square plate with sand in it, and the sixty-millimeter mortar—hand held—sat in it. He got me to run the sixty.

"I saw a couple of holes in the boat, so I knew the people on the beach were not actually blind. The man told me his predecessor got Xed out—not killed, but bent outta shape.

"I asked, 'How often do these shootings happen?'

"He said, 'Oh, once a week. Whenever we go by this spot it happens. Must have been fifteen, twenty times.'

"He had on his flak jacket and helmet. I was running the sixty, and of course I didn't have a flak jacket or a helmet. The Vietnamese guy underneath the waterline had one. I asked, 'Why don't you go into the beach and run those guys out?'

" 'Well,' he said, 'we don't have any troops.'

"I said, 'Get some troops. Go in there and wipe them out. Just go in there and clean house.'

"He said, 'We've got the boats but we don't have any men.'

"A light bulb went on in my head. I said, 'Well, if I had about a hundred and seventy people here, could you do it? Could you get them to the beach?'

"The guy said, 'Are you serious?'

"I said, 'Yeah, man. I'm like Hertz Rent A Company. A company of 'Yards.' We could take off, like we were on a beach party or something. The whole company could disappear for two days. We'd take some trucks like we were going to a beach party—and we'll throw our own war. 'I've got a company up there, and it's not too far away. Can do easy, GI.'

"The guy started thinkin'. 'Well, I got a friend who's got a destroyer.' He told me this destroyer ran up and down the coast and never pulled into port. The minesweepers did. But not the big ships. They helped with gunnery. They'd always been hot to trot, but they never had the opportunity to get in and see people.

"When the lieutenant commander running the minesweeper told the captain of the destroyer, he said, 'Hey, I'd love to. We could meet you down at Song Mau and run you out in the junk boats.' See, he had a very flexible mission of running up and down the coast—unless he was called in for fire support somewhere, and in II Corps there was very little of that.

"I went to Clyde Sincere, who ran the Mike Force then, and borrowed the company. It was just like taking them out for a two-day beer bust.

"Then I went to the 'Yards and said, 'Hey, we're gonna go on a boat ride.' Most of 'em had never seen the ocean. Now we were going to a beach party, bag and baggage, three basic loads. Sincere just turned his head. We had a company plus, a whole menagerie.

"We showed up at Song Mau. Everybody who knew anything about it was kind of lookin' the other way. They didn't think it was going to happen. When we got there, sure enough, there was the captain of the junk force with his little boats.

"Some of the 'Yards who had never seen the ocean ran down and tried to drink the water—and got irate because it was salty. They'd never heard of salt water. They figured the only person low enough to put salt in water would be a Vietnamese. Their concept of water was a creek.

"It was funny later to watch one of them telling somebody in the mountains about the ocean. You know the word for water is *nuk*. He was trying to describe the breakers; '*Nuk nuk nuk nuk* WHOOOM! *Nuk nuk nuk nuk* WHOOOM!' The other guy shook his head. 'Everybody knows there's not that much water in the world. You been hittin' the *numpai* jug, pal.'

"So help me, all this is the truth. Kelley will back me up on this. The guy with the destroyer had a friend who was also captain of a destroyer, and he had nothing else to do and he happened to be going by at the time, so he took half the 'Yards, and the other half went with me. They put the 'Yards on the fantail and the Navy was trying to get rid of all their soup, chicken-noodle soup and crackers, and the 'Yards were eatin' it like it was going out of style.

"Lots of funny things happened. For instance, one little 'Yard came up to me with a five-dollar bill. Some of the guys couldn't read or write, but they knew what size and color money should be. This kid wanted to know, '*Pour-quoi? Changez, mon captaine.*' He'd traded five piasters for five bucks with some sailor who didn't know anything because he'd never been in-country and who wanted a souvenir. The kid didn't want the five-dollar bill; he wanted his five piasters back."

We didn't carry green in-country. No way the Montagnard kid could know that the normal rate of exchange was about one-twenty to one in favor of the dollar. "I reached into my pocket and gave him a five-piaster note. Who was I to make both of them unhappy?

"Of course, there was trading going on. I told the captain of the ship I was on, 'Tomorrow you can trade anything you want. I'll give you my rifle. But I don't want any of these dudes hitting the beach without a rifle or missing a grenade or something.' He put out the word, but they traded on the other ship.

"When we hit the beach the next morning there must have been twenty of my guys with white sailor hats on. It's not that my guys wanted sailor hats, but those sailors were going out of their minds to have tiger fatigue caps for souvenirs.

"And this all started from missing an airplane. The captain of the second destroyer was a lieutenant colonel, what the Navy calls a commander. He came aboard—and they were having their jollies with me. He called me 'Mr. Dring.' So I told 'em the only mister in the Army is a warrant officer. Then they started calling me lieutenant—and I started using the term *colonel*. So I pulled their chain too.

"The destroyer captain started talking about gunfire support. I said, 'What? Hey, there can't be but a platoon of them in there. What do you think this is, the battle of Iwo Jima?'

"He said, 'We're going to open up from ten thousand yards.'

"They were what? This is a scout company. You know, tiptoe through the tulips. I didn't even have a helmet.

"I said, 'If I need you I'll call you.' But they wanted to prep the beach.

"Well, it was a free fire zone. They could do anything they wanted. I couldn't talk them out of it. So the two ships came in turned sideways, and they turned all their tubes to the beach. They started shelling it. First they'd sent the minesweeper into a little cove by the beach. He parked where he could shoot his forty millimeter but still be out of range. Then the two ships picked him up on radar and guided in on him. They profiled the beach and started shootin' VT—variable-time fuses. They were gonna get the guys in the trenches, like they were Japanese or something. You couldn't see a sailor above deck on the beach side. The VT was blowing from the tubes to the beach. It looked like somebody was throwing truckloads of gravel. All the tubes were firing and they were setting each other off.

"The cox'n in my boat said he was gonna run by there. I said, 'Whoa, pal. Cease! Desist! You ain't goin' no place or I'll blow your head off.'

"I got on the radio and said, 'Whoa! Stop the gunfire. You want to shoot HE and WP [high explosives and white phosphorus], have an orgasm, but do not shoot the VT. You're gonna clean me out, pal. I'm not gonna put any of these boats forward until you start shootin' HE or WP.'

"They switched to WP.

"We started forward. Some of the 'Yards got to the front of the little, flat-nosed landing barge and held on to the grate. They really loved it until they hit the surf—then it didn't seem like such a good thing.

"I had an SFC named William T. Mitchell with me, big black guy, he must have been six foot seven. He was good luck—he'd saved my butt on a previous operation. He was good people. Billy Mitchell stepped out of the boat when the ramp went down into water that was about four or five feet high. We were twenty feet from the beach. Suddenly six-foot-seven disappeared. He'd stepped in a chuckhole or a shell hole or something. And they wanted guys who were four foot five to get off there? Nooo!

"Mitchell came back up and moved forward another five feet to where the water was knee deep. But it was still hard to get the other guys out.

"Before we got to the beach, I looked up. I knew we had the minesweeper and two destroyers. But now we had another boat going in with us, dark gray, black letters: U.S. Coast Guard. A Coast Guard cutter. They didn't have anything else to do either. The cutter had a breech-fed eighty-one millimeter on its bow and a dude on the side was firing a twenty mike-mike. He wore an oversized gray helmet, an orange life jacket, a white T-shirt, and a pair of shorts— and was holding a cup of coffee. If you gotta go to war that's the way to do it, with a cup of coffee and a pair of shorts. That Coast Guard cutter took us almost into the beach. It came in almost as far as the landing barges did.

"There were about twenty homegrown VC on the beach. We went in and shot the place up. Resistance was spotty. We pretty well cleaned the place out. It was a little village that had been evacuated. We threw a satchel charge into a cave after a VC. Out came about five hundred bats, but he stayed. There were two wells. We filled 'em up with phosphorus and threw a satchel charge down so the place was no longer usable. The junk boat never got shot at again.

"We got back aboard and returned to the destroyers and then the people really had a good time.

"After two or three weeks I went down to Nha Trang to pick up a payroll for my guys. I got to the S-3 shop. I had a friend there, Master Sergeant Julian C. Haleamau." Holly looked like a cross between a buffalo and a fireplug. He is a taciturn man, and was a legend in Special Forces, not only for bravery, but for common sense. "When I walked in, it dawned on me that it was too quiet. I looked up and everybody was standing at attention.

"There was Splash. He was very unhappy about something or other. I said, 'Uh-oh,' because I wasn't neatly dressed, as usual, and I quietly tried to tiptoe to the rear.

" 'Come here, young Dring!' And he didn't smile at all. 'I want to tell you something.'

"I said, 'What have I done?'

"He said, 'I just got a congratulatory message from MACV. They wanted to congratulate Special Forces on their fine conduct on a combined operation.'

"I was trying to figure out what he was talking about.

" 'Would you know anything about that combined operation?' For the life of me I couldn't figure out what he was talking about. 'Did you take it upon yourself to borrow the United States Navy?'

"And then it sank in. To me it was just a trip to the beach, but the Navy had put it in, and some Air Force guy had flown over, and they'd put it out as a combined operation. The Navy was giving out medals and they wrote it up as the Normandy Invasion.

"Splash started to grin. He said, 'Where did you get the idea for this invasion?'

"I really didn't know what to say. 'Well, sir, I once saw a movie about World War II.'

"That broke him up. He said, 'The next time you borrow the U.S. Navy, at least have the goodness to notify my headquarters ahead of time. I could have got you a medal if I'd known about it.' He could have got me the combined services something or other."

# Médaille Militaire

Dring had plenty of medals; two Silver Stars, four Bronze Stars, the Cambodian Médaille Militaire, and four Vietnamese Crosses of Gallantry. He also had the Soldier's Medal.

"I got that," he said, "for fishin' a couple of guys out of a river one night. Two of my little guys walked off a log into deep water. I went under and stuffed them and their packs and equipment up, hoping that somebody else would get 'em, because I was on the bottom. Then it was my turn and I came up, then I went back under and shoved them up again. Somebody got 'em about the third time."

His Army Commendation Medal with a "V" device, for valor, is another story. Dring told me it happened when a colonel told him, "I'm going to put you in for a Bronze Star."

Dring said, "I told him, 'Thank you.' He looked at me and said, 'You don't seem too happy about it.'

"I said, 'I've never been in a place where I could get an ARCOM. Why don't you put me in for that?'

"It's a lesser decoration, but I told him, 'Look, I already got four of the red ones. This green one would go great with my khakis.' "

Dring also has five Purple Hearts. He told me, "I was one of the first fifty guys to get a Purple Heart in Vietnam.

President Kennedy letter orders. That's had my records screwed up because there's no order number from the unit. It's a letter order from the President. I was a staff sergeant when I got it. They had a big ceremony at Fort Buckner, Okinawa. The general gave it to me. He pinned it on and said, 'Well, Sergeant, I'm sure glad to be giving this to you rather than your parents.'

"I said, 'Me too.'

"I got into a fight with a Marine over that Heart, because at the time there was no campaign ribbon for it. All I had was a Good Conduct Medal and a Purple Heart.

"The Marine asked, 'Where were you?'

" 'Vietnam.'

"He wanted to know where that was. I said, 'You go to China and turn left and you'll run right into it.' He didn't believe me."

# Unusual Romance

Larry had two kids, both carbon copies of their father—
God help us—and his wife Becky was the missionary nurse
I had heard about. I asked them about their unusual ro-
mance:

"It all started when we"—he and his Mike Force Company—"were out on patrol on Christmas. We were over the
border during that phony truce. I reported that we knocked
off ten of 'em on Christmas—the twenty-fifth of December
was just another day. They shot at us and we shot back.

"Headquarters got real indignant about it and pulled us
back in. It was a truce; they told us, but they forgot to tell
the other guys. Headquarters said, 'Aw, ya violated the
truce. Blah, blah, blah, blah.'

"So we got back to the Mike Force compound at II Corps
headquarters, Pleiku, and I was the only guy there who had
his whole company together. Major Justin McCarthy, the
CO, said, 'Hey, will you ask your guys to fill in?' It might
seem odd to have to ask 'em. . . ." You don't usually have
to negotiate with troops to get them to accept a mission,
but our Strike Forces were legally civilians. "But we'd
make deals—contract with them. Most Americans never
understood that we contracted for missions. McCar-

thy made us an offer, 'Okay, you keep 'em together for Tet and we'll give you a week and a half off.'

"I said, 'Okay, can do.' We were ready. We had three basic loads of ammo in our packs. We were heavy on grenades. We'd just come from Bong Son, and the place is full of caves, trenches, and ditches—all that stuff, and were carrying four frags and a couple of phosphorus each. I'd usually have the guys fill an extra canteen cover with five grenades and hang it off their belts to the rear.

"On the morning of the thirtieth, about four-thirty or five A.M., the sector advisor called from Pleiku and said, 'Hey, there's some small-arms fire coming from the vicinity of the POW compound.' " Which was just off the main road into Pleiku from the Special Forces compound. "We were out maybe three miles from town on the high plains. A couple of miles further out was the MACV complex of villas—palatial, but insecure—and a CIA school for village cadre.

"We were operating our radios off the Military Assistance Advisory Group (MAAG) frequency—the only one I had. They said, 'Do not—do not—take machine guns, mortars, or rockets, because you're just going downtown. You'll be back by noon. Maybe put a can of CS tear gas in your pocket or something like that.'

"So we bopped down to Pleiku. We went by the POW compound—no action, just POW's snoozin'. Then I heard what I thought was gunfire, coming out of the New Pleiku area." There was the old section, and the new market section which had grown out toward our camp. "I had about 170 tribesmen in my company."

I said, "That's a big bunch of guys for a CIDG company."

Dring answered, "I had a pretty fat company. I always had volunteers. I never had to go lookin' for people because they'd come to me. The 'Yards wouldn't go out with some of the other guys—and I'd be out sometimes with almost two companies.

"They'd come marchin' in in platoon formation," he said, explaining that his troops were members of FULRO, the Montagnard revolutionary organization. Most of them had been trained as soldiers in Special Forces camps and then left our service. Sometimes they fought alone in the jungle, and sometimes—when they needed money—they'd fight for the Americans for a while, "and I'd just accept 'em. They'd come marchin' in barefoot—but in columns of fours. They'd say, 'This guy's the platoon leader, this other guy's the platoon sergeant.' I'd accept that.

'Some of the other advisers wanted to direct traffic. I'd tell them, 'Hey, you gotta go by the lay of the land. You gotta go by what the people think. If they say, 'Hey, this guy's the leader,' he's the leader. Why try to make him a corporal?

"So we got down to the POW compound and I heard what I thought was gunfire. I started deploying into combat formation.

"I noticed something. These clowns—about one per block—were shootin' firecrackers all over the town. 'Course, during Tet you expect people to be shootin' firecrackers. But after being over there five tours you start learning the customs. Normally they'd shoot strings of small firecrackers. But these were loud singles—they sounded almost like gunshots. In fact, that was the purpose of the exercise.

"When you pop a firecracker there's a little bit of paper on the ground. But I started lookin' and thinkin', that's an awful lot of paper, and an awful lot of noise. Something was wrong. I didn't know what, but there was something wrong about those firecrackers.

"Then I started hearing, every now and then, *popop . . . popop . . . popop*. The guys that were doing it were very good, because they were keeping it down. The firecrackers were masking it, but every now and then I'd hear one just a little bit too close. And I said, 'Forsooth! That's gunfire.'

"So I started aimin' my men toward the missionary compound, because I knew the people there. In fact, I was pretty familiar with the town. The II Corps spook place, the CIA, was right next to the missionaries' compound, and that's where they had all their intelligence agents' names filed.

"You know the way Pleiku is—the streets are laid out in strips, and one group of houses faces one way and the other faces out, back to back, with a communal back wall and no break between houses in the block. There's usually only one door to the house and it faces the street, so you can't go over somebody's back fence. You have to go to the corner; it channels your unit.

"Another thing: If you held the mission compound, you could shoot straight down the street and X anybody that tried to go across. We got there at about five thirty, quarter to six in the morning. The town ends at the mission compound, which is in the last row of houses. There's nothing but rice fields and a little brush beyond it.

"And right there, across the street, were more VC—no, North Vietnamese regulars—than I'd ever seen in any one place, including the POW compound, during five tours in 'Nam. The squad leaders were getting their people on line, getting ready to sweep through.

"We found out later they'd been told that the Vietnamese military were gone, that it was gonna be a walk-through. They were gonna meet up with those firecrackers guys, who would give 'em the names, telling 'em who to knock off and who to leave alone, just like Hue." In Hue during Tet '68, the NVA executed over two thousand government sympathizers, military or civilian, men, women, children. It made no difference. "They'd been told the people were gonna rise up and be with 'em and all that stuff.

"Then we showed up on the other side of the street, no more than twenty meters away. I looked across the street at them—I was in front so I got a pretty good show. Picture it—you have a rifle and you're lookin' at some guys across the street. You could throw a rock and kill 'em. You're used to seein' 'em at about a hundred meters.

"And they looked at us and we looked at them and then—wow! WHAM! WHAM! PING! It started raining bullets.

"I looked over again and the first thing I saw across the street, sitting in a small courtyard—most of the houses had them—was a little old gray-haired lady and a couple of kids.

"So I yelled to the 'Yard platoon leader, *'Regardez la femme! Non grenade!* There's a woman over there.'

"I'd just gotten the words out of my mouth when—WHAM! I got hit with a grenade. Little dude chucked one at me and caught me in the back. It redesigned me; I mean it put holes in me. I was saved because I didn't like plastic canteens. They made the water taste lousy, and I didn't like aluminum ones because they corroded, so I had a steel one."

"Jeez," I said, "I haven't seen one of those for years."

"It was an old World War Twice steel one, and I had a steel cup. The biggest slug hit me in the spine, later causing me a lot of grief. It went through the canteen, cup and cover, and if I'd had a plastic one it would have come right out my stomach.

"It knocked me down. I had a piece coming out of my head and my back was torn up, and I was lying there, not feeling too happy. And I looked up and saw this little gerbil with an AK and he just laid it on me. It was like a fistfight. You see the fist comin' and you know you could be hurt—then there's that little gut feeling that says, 'You *are* gonna be hurt.'

"This guy went WHAM! and it was the most painful thing that ever happened to me. He blew out six inches of femoral artery. I thought, 'Boy! He hit me in the leg. But if he can't shoot any better'n that . . .'

"As he went by me, I grabbed my M1A1 carbine and flipped it over like a pistol and *plup . . . plup . . . plup*. I got a little equal time there.

"My medic came out to get me, an old gray-haired Chinese guy. And he took one, a shot just under the jaw—we didn't have flak jackets or helmets. It removed the top of his head and he lay there . . . and he wriggled a little bit.

"Then my radioman came out. He still had his radio on.

"Remember, these were people I'd been with for five years. I'd been over to their homes and knew their families. The radioman came out to get me and they hit him with a B-40 rocket and he just disappeared.

"I lay there and this American tank came whizzing up. I thought the dumb PFC in the turret was gonna run me over. I found out later he was the platoon leader. I yelled, "FIRE!" He had more firepower than my entire company. He could have wiped 'em out.

"He looked down at me like, *What are you?* That guy didn't get one round off. Not a round. They hit the tank. Wham! Wham! Wham! Wham!

"There were four guys in there. Two of 'em got out and two of 'em stayed. They started throwin' baggage out. Two Americans still in that tank and this guy's worried about baggage. Eventually the tank cooked off and a twelve-ton turret went up through the air like a lollipop.

"About then somebody grabbed me by the suspenders and dragged me into the nearest house. He kicked the door open and—wow! Four nurses and a doctor. No sign on the door, but they were missionaries and they lived in that house. One nurse was Becky. There were about ten of us in there with her. Of course I'd seen her in church a couple of times, but I'd never really talked to her before.

"I didn't even have the wherewithal to mash on a handset. I had her hold the handset for me and I said, 'Mash,' and I snapped. Man, there were MAAGots on there asking, 'What's going on?' You know. It was a MACV frequency for the whole Pleiku area. And those dudes were busy talkin' to each other. 'What's goin' on?'

"I got a little unhappy about the whole thing. I guess I upset a few people. I found out some guy was just sittin' in a bunker at the end of the runway, curious about what was goin' on. So I said, 'You sorry———people.' "

I told him that probably wasn't what he said.

Dring admitted, "Well, I got a little unhappy. The only guy who understood what was going on was McCarthy. I couldn't believe it.

I said, 'There's a reinforced company down here. We've bitten off more than we can chew.' They hijacked two American tanks and a Mike Force company—because a second tank had arrived, but it knew how to operate. You know, run over the house and shoot.

"While I was inside the rest of my guys were being literally blown back across the street into those little houses. It was like a whole bunch of Alamos. They couldn't get out because there was no back door, but the NVA couldn't get across the street to get in, either, no matter how many of them there were.

"I think it was the phosphorus that saved as many of us as survived. The frag goes bang, makes a lot of noise, but you don't see it. But phosphorus, you start slinging that around and guys want to run back across the street." White phosphorus makes smoke, and a nice fireworks display. It will also burn right through almost anything, especially people.

"We were like the Dutch boy with his finger in the dike, but we had to bleed for it. Of four advisers, one was killed and three wounded.

"I found out later that those guys with the firecrackers did have lists. They were gettin' ready to go around and knock people off. They were Viet Cong that were comin' out of the woodwork. Our side aced out the Viet Cong in Pleiku, because they surfaced. All we had to do was locate those houses that had firecracker paper around them, because you can't pick up all that paper quickly. Most of the Vietnamese in Pleiku weren't home. They were visiting other places. But the guys who stayed at home shootin' firecrackers, they were Cong, the real VC infrastructure."

Becky, who had been sitting beside Larry, said, "I went over in September 1967 and left the following February. Right around Christmas, and from then on we heard there was going to be an attack on the city and that if we stayed in our house everything would be okay. But as Tet got nearer we got more concerned.

"One night we woke up and heard gunfire out in front of our house. We had one central room that had no windows at all, and we went there. Finally one of the guys got brave and went to find out what was going on.

"We lived on one side of the house, and Chinese lived on the other. There was a walkway between the main part of the house and the dining room, and there was a walk between each section.

"The wounded were dragged in there. I don't like heights, but I climbed the wall and went over there to take care of the wounded. I went into the front room and Larry was one of them. And I thought, *Oh, I've seen him before, at the hymn sing.*"

I asked, "How bad was he dinged?"

"He had about six inches of artery missing from his right leg. His leg was wide open."

"Tourniquet?" I asked.

Dring answered, "Not at that time."

Becky said, "A medic, or someone, outside, had stuffed in wadding of some sort; otherwise he would have bled to death. He was on a mattress, and they dragged him to the back section, where the kitchen and dining room were. I helped take care of him.

"Then people came in and said a tank with a full load of ammunition and fuel had been hit outside, so we should get out. We climbed the walls of the compound and went into the houses in back of us. No one was there.

"We found out later that those people had known what was going on, because there was a whole tunnel system right across the street from our house; there was so much underbrush, you couldn't see it.

"Soon they asked for a volunteer to go back and take care of the wounded. I went and stayed until we were evacuated. Soon a doctor came in and we started plasma and stuff like that.

"When we were evacuated, we were taken to the Special Forces compound for part of the day, and then we were taken to the hospital, which gave us one ward. They needed help, so all of our nurses helped 'em. What really amazed me was that there were North Vietnamese wounded in our hospital. And, boy, did they act nasty. I don't think they would have done as much for us as we did for them.

"The next morning some of the people in our group thought we should go back to help the wounded in town. I wasn't too crazy about it, but I thought, *All right, if you want to we'll go back.*

"I drove a Korean vintage jeep, rode right up and over barbed wire and kept going. Someone told me later we were fortunate the jeep didn't stop right there. The Vietnamese people didn't want to associate with us, because if the enemy came back they could be killed too. So we were there long enough to get some clothes and pack a suitcase and go up to the clinic. Someone said the North Vietnamese were coming back—get outa town. I never went back.

"We got back to the hospital and I said, 'Let's go see Larry.' I grabbed one of my friends and we went over to intensive care and found him. I went to see him every day until he was evacuated.

"At that time he proposed. I accepted."

Dring said that wasn't the whole story. "I was in a long ward, and most of the people on it were my people. What was left of the guys from the Mike Force. A couple of guys got together. They wanted to do something nice for me.

"So they got an Australian go-go girl to put on a performance. That was when Becky showed up. I thought, *How in the world am I gonna explain this?*

"So I said, 'Thank you very much, but Becky's the one I want to talk to.'

"My old Mike Force commander, Major McCarthy, came by and gave me a .45. He said that one of the guys we bumped off was a battalion executive officer who had an ops order that said the next target was the hospital. They'd already shelled it, taken out the pharmacy, a nurse, and a couple of corpsmen. So McCarthy gave me his .45 and two magazines.

"Along came a nurse major. She said, 'Oh, you can't have a gun.'

"I said, 'Lady, this could be a very bad scene.'

" 'Well,' she said, 'we have these two corpsmen to protect you.' Two dudes, very nice people, white uniforms, helmets, flak jackets—and one M14 with one magazine.

"I said, 'Lady, about four kilometers down that road I lost a rifle company.' She thought I misplaced it.

"I kept trying to explain what the word *lost* meant, but I couldn't get the message across. I had a lanyard around my neck and I had that .45 hooked to it.

"So I said, 'Huh-uh! I'm not givin' it up. I'll be very nice, but what are you gonna do to me, shoot me? Send me to Vietnam?' She got all upset.

"She had another girl come in later and hit me with Demerol. I woke up without the .45, but I still had the lanyard around my neck and two magazines under my pillow.

"For three days during Tet they couldn't get anybody out during the daytime. At night they'd orbit a C-130. The aircraft would come in; it wouldn't even cut the engine, but come in, drop the ramp, and they'd start chuckin' litters on. When the rockets started comin' in they'd up the ramp and book it. After about three days they could bring 'em in in the daytime and it started levelin' out.

"I was there for eleven days.

"On a couple of nights Becky and I went outside. It was just like The Star-Spangled Banner; 'Rockets' red glare, bombs bursting in air.' That tickled me.

"It was comical; the people who were bedridden, who couldn't get out, had a mattress over them like a sandwich. The rest of the people were put under the bed. I just took the mattress off. If they were gonna get me they were gonna get me. The mattress was a bore. I guess I wasn't the world's best patient. I tried to be nice.

"I proposed to her on the medEvac aircraft just before it left, when she came up the ramp to say good-bye."

# Operation Barroom

Down there in the Georgia pines at Fort Benning, officer candidates are taught to "think positive." "Make a bold move" is one maxim drummed into their open and receptive young heads. "Doing something is better than doing nothing" is another.

Therefore it is not surprising that when one of our lieutenants was asked over the phone by a USAID rep in Saigon, "If USAID buys elephants for the Tra Bong sawmill, can y'all move them?" he replied, "Sure, baby! We'll move your elephants."

When the full ramifications of the elephant story came to light this young officer could not be identified, and did not come forward. This exemplifies another maxim, dear to staff officers: "Cover your ass." Clearly this young man was assured of a brilliant military career.

Captain J. Scott Gantt's emaciated but limber body splayed across his swivel chair in the Special Forces headquarters. An expression both sardonic and baffled played across his face as he cocked an eyebrow and inquired, "Whuffo we want to move elephants to Tra Bong?"

The question was directed at Master Sergeant Robert Bennett. Bennett, the noncommissioned officer in charge of what was called "Revolutionary Development", the then-current buzzword for our nation-building efforts, resembled an uncompassionate Buddha, smiling smugly, fingers laced across his kettledrum belly as he swiveled his chair back and forth in quick, nervous movements. "The Tra Bong sawmill cooperative is a joint civic action project between our "A" team there and USAID," he said. "It is the sole support of two hundred Montagnard families who have moved in around the camp for security. They have cut down all the logs close enough to the mill to haul, and the ground is too rough and hilly for machinery. Hence elephants."

Captain Gantt stretched like a lazy lizard and ambled into the junior officer cage to visit handsome First Lieutenant Roy T. "Sweet Roy" Kimbrough, beloved of young women on three continents.

"Roy," he said, "lay on a convoy to haul elephants, four each, two to go to Tra Bong, and two to Kham Duc. We pick up the elephants in Ban Me Thuot, truck them here, load them on an LST for Da Nang, and walk them overland to the camps. Okay?"

Kimbrough looked up and flared his nostrils, in the dramatic way that made the hearts of young ladies flutter when he did it in their presence. "Roger," he said, and reached for the telephone, then paused and looked up. "What they eat?" he inquired innocently.

"Hmmm," said Gantt. "Maybe we better find out."

"Fifty pounds of high-grade hay per day per ton of elephant, plus fifty gallons of water per day per elephant. At three tons of elephant per each for four elephants, times nine days, that's about 5,400 pounds of hay, plus 1,800 gallons of water. You'll need one LST for the elephants and another for chow. Plus the elephants may get very seasick. I suggest we try for air movement."

These words were spoken by Captain Tommy Dees of Edenton, North Carolina, the group vet, a Huck Finn clone in a green beret. He leaned in the doorway with a book on elephants by Frank Buck open in his hand, and another by L. Sprague DeCamp tucked under his arm.

"Incidentally, the closest source of this hay is Manila." He spoke with a thick southern accent.

"The roads from the camp are too insecure to move overland," Kimbrough put in. "And we can't airland at Tra Bong. The strip is too short. How we gonna get them in?"

Sergeant Richard Campbell, who had been following all this wearing a bemused expression, said, "Airdrop?"

Dees blinked, held up two fingers in the Churchill salute, said, "Peace in Veet Namm," turned, and walked off down the hall.

While the purchase of elephants was nothing new for Special Forces, an attempt to air-move them was. So Gantt called the Air Force. He was informed the only aircraft in Vietnam that could handle the move was a C-130. Since the strip at Tra Bong was too small to land a 130—Kham Duc had plenty of runway—they would have to land at Da Nang. And they couldn't be moved by land from Da Nang.

There were other difficulties with the Air Force. They were glad to move the elephants, but had very stringent regulations about the air movement of large animals. The Air Force was leery of elephants crashing around inside the cargo bay in flight, adversely affecting the trim of the aircraft. Having once seen a C47 full of Somerset pigs unloaded in Pleiku I didn't blame them.

Their requirement was that the elephants had to be unconscious and strapped down like cargo. In addition, in case one woke up, a weapon big enough to kill an elephant had to be mounted inside the aircraft. The smallest weapon in the military inventory capable of taking out an elephant quickly and simply was a .50 caliber machine gun, so one of these would also have to be mounted inside the aircraft.

As to Campbell's suggestion that they be air-dropped, a

quick call to the rigger section verified that it was indeed feasible to drop something that size and weight. The rigger sergeant suggested that five hundred-foot cargo chutes per elephant would do the job.

Dees, a qualified parachutist as well as a veterinarian, agreed the elephants could take the drop if they were strapped down on cargo pallets and the pallets mounted on stacks of honeycomb shock absorbers, a device commonly used in air-dropping heavy machinery.

While all of this was in the planning stage, it became an in-Group joke, christened "Operation Barroom" after the punch line of a gag about an elephant fart, and rumors of the upcoming airdrop started floating around Vietnam.

Gantt got inquiries from curious reporters. That was when I, as Information Officer, was called in.

A claim on the story was more or less staked out by John MacLennan of Reuters, and Curt Rolffes of UPI. MacLennan was a South African, a big, easygoing guy who, except for his costume, looked almost exactly like Captain Marvel. Normally he wore U.S. Army fatigues with a patch that said CORRESPONDENT.

Rolffes was a tall, dark-haired fellow, a photographer who had done a spell as a Peace Corps volunteer. He wore one of the world's most spectacular beard-and-mustache combinations. The beard came to two points below his chin. The mustache looked like rabbit-ears antennae, no less than seven inches on a side, waxed to needle points, quivering at the ends, which were more or less even with his eyeballs. I knew Rolffes from a great shot in *Stars and Stripes*, of him in his beard and moustache, staring bug-eyed and cross-eyed at one of his cameras that had taken a round right through the camera body.

They wanted to know did we really plan to air-drop the elephants? MacLennan called Gantt on the phone and was given an enthusiastic reply, full of positive-sounding noises.

We really did want to. Paratroopers are kind of funny

anyway and we wanted to prove that it could be done. However, after MacLennan's first story, ominous rumbles came from the British SPCA and it looked like we would get an awful lot of flak if one of the chutes malfunctioned and we splattered elephant all over Tra Bong.

Alternate plan B had to be developed. The Marines in I Corps were willing to provide a couple of choppers. We would sling-load the elephants on cargo pallets under the helicopters and take them from Chu Lai to Tra Bong.

"Do you definitely plan to air-drop the elephants?" John MacLennan asked. Hovering nearby was his buddy Rolffes, the UPI photographer, in his luxuriant beard and mustache.

"Only as a last resort," Gantt said. "We are going to try to lift them by flying crane from Da Nang to Tra Bong. Kham Duc's no problem, because we can air-land there.

"The thing is, we have to airlift these elephants in crates. If we just try to sling them under the crane, the weight of their bodies will crush the elephants' diaphragm, killing them."

"But, I say," MacLennan asked, "won't the elephants tend to thrash about a bit?"

"Oh, they'll be tranquilized," Gantt answered confidently.

MacLennan and Rolffes were not highly pleased with alternate plan B, since it was not nearly as spectacular a story.

Dees had an animal tranquilizer in stock, which the Group had used occasionally to move animals as large as water buffalo. But by conservative estimate it would require 240 cc of this stuff to knock out an elephant. These tranquilizers were administered by firing a hypodermic dart from an air rifle into the behind of the animal. The capacity of the darts is 10 cc. No one knew of any elephants sufficiently placid to stand still while they were shot in the ass by twenty-four darts. Another tranquilizer had to be found.

• • •

"You're calling from where?" the operator asked, incredulously.

"Vietnam, ma'am," Gantt replied. "I want to talk to the Cleveland Zoo." It was hard for him to keep the edge out of his voice. He had been on the phone for a little over eleven hours, and had talked to three different zoos trying to locate the right tranquilizer for the elephants. Dees was on the extension, both feet propped up on Sergeant Bennett's desk, phone cradled in his neck. He had all the paper clips in the dish on Bennett's desk linked into a chain seven feet in circumference and was starting to work on a string of paper dolls.

The first hour was spent trying to explain to military operators, who must have justification, that the 5th Special Forces Group (Airborne) had a valid reason for wanting to discuss elephant tranquilization with someone twelve thousand miles away, in the States.

Finally he got through to Cleveland. He was informed that an experimental drug had been tested in Africa, a high-intensity morphine derivative, which could knock out any elephant known, in under ten seconds.

"Yessir, yessir," he said, fighting the sleep in his bones, furiously scribbling notes. "The name of the drug is M-99 and it's manufactured by Reckitts and Sons. Where is Reckitts and Sons?" He paused to listen to the reply. When it came, the pencil dropped from his fingers and he laid his head down on the desk, slowly beating on it with his left fist.

Dees whistled a long, low whistle. When the conversation was over he said, "Well, it took us twelve hours to call the States. You wanta wait till tomorrow to call Hull, England?"

"Yeah," Gantt replied. "We'll wait until tomorrow, or

maybe even the day after. Is the bar closed yet?"

"Yep," said Dees. "Gawd! England!"

They made the call to England from my shop, where we put out the Group magazine and had a number of phones, so they could both talk. I listened on an extension. Damndest thing I ever heard. First the call had to be relayed through Saigon, then Honolulu, San Francisco, Washington, New York, the French city of Navarre, and a couple of others. The last voice we heard was the operator in Bristol, England, saying, "Wheah? Viet-Nayam?" We couldn't hear Hull and had to relay through the Bristol operator.

The upshot of the conversation was that Recketts and Sons had the drug and it was everything claimed. All the 5th Special Forces had to do was procure a narcotics import license through the Walter Reed Army Medical Center and we were in business.

That took about six weeks.

By the time the change from airdrop to air move had been announced, the British SPCA was picketing the American embassy in London and stories like the following appeared in the British press:

A HEAVY PROTEST ON "ELEPHANT DROP"
by London Express Service

London, Jan 18—Authoress Mabel Raymond-Hawkins deals with hundreds of animal problems at her 68-acre Sussex Animal Welfare Centre—"anything from hamsters to horses."

When she heard about the elephant drop into Vietnam, Mrs. Raymond-Hawkins, 65, stormed into the U.S. embassy in London with a "jumbo" sized complaint.

"It's completely inhuman," the lady protested, "to

parachute four 5-ton elephants in crates into thick
Vietnam jungle."

Said Mrs. Raymond-Hawkins: "I'm not a woolly
sentimentalist about animals. I can look a dead elephant in the face—but not a maimed one.

"Their poor pillar-like legs would take a terrible
jar.

"This has nothing to do with my feeling about the
war," she said. "A sense of justice is involved. Justice
for elephants—and I'm on their side."

"They're rioting in London about the elephants, and the
British Society for the Prevention of Cruelty to Animals is
sending a delegation to protest our cruel and inhumane
treatment of them. We got a call from the embassy last
night," said Doc Tsoulis, the Group surgeon.

"That certainly puts this whole protest business in perspective," Gantt said, now completely numb to shock.

"When you gonna drop the elephants?" Doc asked.

"Air-move, not air-drop. Please don't say air-drop. I
don't want to ever hear those two words in that particular
sequence again." His face was gray.

"Air-move then?"

"As soon as the M-99 gets here."

After a cable from the State Department, without consulting
me, Gantt, or anybody else in Group, a U.S. embassy
spokesman inaccurately explained the "jumbo drop" to the
press. In their version two of the four elephants flown to
Vietnam would be carried in nets slung underneath helicopters and landed at their "thick jungle destinations." No
parachuting was involved.

*The elephants would help Vietnamese to rebuild villages
destroyed by bombing.*

There were no bombed-out villages near Tra Bong. We

were not trying to correct a mistake; we were just trying to help people.

Many people in the States, perhaps most, believed the U.S. was killing off thousands of innocent people, that Vietnam was an eroding wasteland. There was massive social dislocation attributable to the war, but we had stringent rules of engagement designed to avoid civilian casualties. We *lost* a lot of guys because of those rules, tens of thousands.

It was my hope that this elephant story would give us the hook we needed to make the point that the U.S. was going to elaborate lengths to help the Vietnamese.

On the same day the *London Express* story came out, Gantt received the following telegram from the State Department:

REQUESTED AMOUNTS OF TRANQUILIZER AND ANTIDOTE FOR ELEPHANTS ARE BEING HELD BY U.S. ARMY MEDICAL SUPPLY CONTROL BRANCH AT WALTER REED ARMY MEDICAL CENTER PENDING COMPLETION OF REQUIRED FORMS BY FIFTH SPECIAL FORCES VIETNAM REGARDING INTENDED USE OF DRUGS, AS REQUIRED BY BUREAU OF NARCOTICS. DRUGS FOR OPERATION BAH-ROOM WILL BE SENT AS SOON AS FORMS RETURNED. RUSK.

All we had to do was wait.

Scott Gantt, meantime, had been to Ban Me Thuot twice to arrange for purchase of the elephants. The procedure was not like buying a used car. First he had to find a Montagnard village with elephants they were willing to sell. It seemed that over a period of years the elephants became part of the family, and they could not be sold except to family friends, and then only after the seller was assured they would be well taken care of. It took Gantt several visits to establish this, and then only because he was in the company of Mike Benge of USAID, who had a close relationship with the tribes.

Finally arrangements were made, the elephants bought and paid for, although remaining in the custody of their original owners. The narcotics import license was received and the drugs were on the way. The project seemed assured of success.

Then came the Tet offensive.

Ban Me Thuot was hit badly during Tet and the elephants ran off during the battle. We had to have new elephants.

It took Gantt an additional two weeks to procure more elephants from Ban Don, another Montagnard village near Special Forces Camp Trang Phuc. He had to do it himself this time: Mike Benge, a civilian, was captured during Tet and spent the next seven years in Hanoi as a POW.

The narcotics arrived and I accompanied him to Ban Don to test the drug. It was powerful stuff; he had to wear a gas mask while firing the air rifle. One of the earlier users of M-99 had inhaled fumes from the drug during testing and died instantly.

So, wearing the gas mask, Gantt fired the first dart into an elephant's rump. He stood back a safe distance and the dart hit crooked and broke off, failing to pierce the elephant's hide. He moved in closer and fired again. Ten seconds later the elephant was out on the ground. It slept like a baby for better than four hours, waking with no apparent ill effects. The stuff worked beautifully.

Tommy Dees had extended his tour in Vietnam twice to insure that the move went off okay. But his time in the Army ended and he was due to start graduate work in microbiology at the University of North Carolina. He went home. We were without a veterinarian. More waiting. Finally the new group vet, a big shambling captain named Stu McCahan, arrived.

He needed time to become acquainted with the problem before supervising the move. More time elapsed.

Finally everything was arranged. The drug was on hand. The vet was on hand. The elephants were on hand. The aircraft were scheduled for the move and the Marine helicopters were scheduled from Chu Lai to Tra Bong. Gantt went to Saigon to supervise things from that end and come back with the aircraft. I sent my assistant, First Lieutenant Frank Orians, with him to arrange for press coverage. Every major wire service and TV network wanted to cover the move. Most of the papers were ready, as well as the news magazines.

The flight was canceled. A nervous Air Force lieutenant colonel said it would *look bad in the press* if the aircraft were scheduled for a noncombat flight when the entire country was still on alert after Tet.

There was no other requirement for the aircraft during the time they were to be used to move the elephants. But this fellow was shaky about it and the flight was canceled. He told Gantt that his flight had been canceled "by the ambassador."

I do not know how Gantt managed it. It must have been difficult for a lowly captain. Conversely, an aroused Special Forces officer is hard to say no to. Thirty minutes later Gantt was standing in front of Ambassador Ellsworth Bunker's desk, demanding to know why "the ambassador" had canceled his aircraft to move his elephants of dubious ancestry and personal habits.

Mr. Bunker replied that he didn't know anything about any elephants, and since the U.S. had an abundance of ambassadors in Vietnam, why didn't Gantt toddle over to Komer's office and ask him about it.

As it turned out Ambassador Robert Komer, the boss of the American side of Revolutionary Development—our effort to rebuild the nation in the midst of destroying it—had indeed canceled the aircraft.

One of Komer's assistants, another Air Force lieutenant colonel, was all for rescheduling the aircraft. He called the original Air Force lieutenant colonel at Ton Son Nhut Air Base and authorized it. But this man was so shaky, he insisted on the ambassador's personal authority.

Komer was pretty busy at the time. His pacification program was in a shambles in the wake of Tet and he was running around the country trying to patch it up. The Air Force lieutenant colonel in Komer's office believed enough in the value of the elephants that he bearded Komer, who breezed through for a change of socks and some more papers before hopping on another airplane, and tried to get him to see Gantt.

Ambassador Komer was a man widely admired for many sterling qualities, but tact and patience were not prominent among them. His final comment as he flung out of the office was "I haven't got time to talk about fucking elephants."

Gantt, I am told, had to be forcibly restrained from killing him.

The long process of getting the elephants scheduled had to be started again. I left Orians to handle that story and went on up north to go into the A Shau Valley with Project Delta. When the elephant story finally did break I was in the 22nd Surgical Hospital with a big hunk of my right arm shot off.

In any case, the Air Force was sort of embarrassed by their previous inability to cooperate and they were quite helpful about rescheduling aircraft. Once again it was all laid on. The aircraft were scheduled. The Marine helicopters were scheduled.

But the movement was canceled again, this time by one Major General McLaughlin, the head logistician in Vietnam. As usual the reason was that it would look bad in the press if noncombat moves were made during the emergency.

However, the next day a story appeared over a Reuters—MacLennan's agency—credit line, telling the story of the elephants and the fact that the Army had canceled the move because of fear of adverse publicity. The upshot of the story was that if the elephants were not delivered, the people of Tra Bong would have no means of livelihood and would have to return to the jungle, under control of the Viet Cong, which was true. The story made McLaughlin look like an ass.

Who leaked the story to the press I don't know. I would have been happy to, but I was in the hospital at Phu Bai. Gantt swears he didn't do it.

The move, entire and complete, was accomplished the next day.

No fewer than twenty-eight members of the press were on hand. In fact extra aircraft were scheduled to move them. Represented were ABC-TV, AP, BBC, CBS-TV, GGTV (Japan), NBC-TV, *Newsweek*, Reuters, *Sydney Daily News, Time*, and UPI.

Dubbed Bonnie and Clyde by the reporters, the two elephants made a fine funny story in a war with little to be humorous about. From an Information Officer's viewpoint it was one that couldn't be better.

But Dr. Martin Luther King was assassinated the day the elephants were moved and nobody ran any funny Vietnam stories that week.

Apparently the Viet Cong had followed the story fairly closely, though, because a large body of them were ambushed the next day moving toward Tra Bong; three were killed. The day after one of the elephants ran away.

# Project Delta

Project Delta, Special Forces Detachment B-52, one of the most highly decorated units in the Vietnam War, was organized in early 1964 under Captain William R. Richardson. Its mission was to provide strategic reconnaissance for MACV. Under the original concept there were no Americans on Delta's recon teams, and the earliest infiltrations were night static-line and High-Altitude-Low-Opening free-fall parachute jumps.

The concept of using only indigenous troops proved unworkable because of operational procedures adopted by the Vietnamese teams, odd habits such as sleeping on the trail where Charlie could find them, and the fanciful nature of some of their reports. It was only six months before American "advisors" started accompanying the patrols.

There were many refinements in Project Delta's operational techniques through the six years of its existence, but the project achieved its highest degree of perfection—and Delta was as close to perfection as anything in war ever is—under Major (later Lieutenant Colonel) Chuck Allen, who was with the project for two years and commanded it for six months. He is the man General William C. Westmoreland called "Big 'Un."

For a time MACV headquarters insisted that recon teams

be commanded by officers, because they did not trust the quality of information received from the enlisted swine. This was an erroneous notion because, for one thing, Special Forces had, at least at that time, enlisted men with, on the average, higher IQs than their officers. And those young lieutenants were a whole lot more flighty than a seasoned SF NCO—which is not to say that the officers were dumb. SF was simply an organization of very bright, dedicated, and ballsy individuals.

In fact, intellectual requirements for Special Forces were exactly the same as those for OCS. The only different requirements were that you had to be able to swim to get into the Forces and you couldn't have a criminal record and get into OCS.

Of those officer recon-team leaders, incidentally, one of the few to work out was Bill Larabee, at the time of my outing with them a captain, Chuck Allen's operations officer.

Because of the success of Delta, Colonel Francis J. "Splash" Kelley formed Projects Sigma and Omega. There are various versions of how that came about. Chuck Allen says that Kelley wanted to use Delta in I Corps and formed Omega for II Corps and Sigma for III Corps. And, as it turned out, that is how they were generally deployed.

But one of my old sergeant buddies told me that early in his tour Kelley was invited down to the Project for dinner. It was a spirited evening; the gentlemen of the Project were well known for their iron discipline and control in the field, and their lack of those qualities in garrison.

As rumor has it, during the course of the evening a master sergeant gave the new colonel a fat, wet kiss on the ear and murmured to him, "Don't ever die, you sweet motherfucker. Don't you even catch cold." It was not unusual for recon men to test an officer's cool in this fashion. Babysan Davidson, a legendary recon NCO, who looked like a demented twelve-year-old, once, at a similar party, kissed me on the ear and murmured, "Y'know, motherfucker, I like you."

I was flattered; junior SF officers were middlin' arrogant, but the recon guys were superstars. According to the story I heard, though, Kelley was not so pleased, and organized his new recon projects the next day.

Under Allen, and thereafter, the core of the Project consisted of the recon section, with twelve teams of ten members each, usually four Americans and six Vietnamese Special Forces men, usually only six of whom were deployed at a time. The headquarters was SF Det B-52. Nominally, the Project was commanded by a Viet lieutenant colonel and Allen was his adviser. The reaction force was the Vietnamese 91st Airborne Ranger Battalion, an organization which had its good points and its not-so-good points. That was why there was also a platoon of Nungs—a Chinese tribe with a mercenary heritage—for bomb-damage assessment. The Nungs, you see, were trained, fed, paid, and led by Americans.

There was also a section of all-Vietnamese teams, known as Roadrunners, which ran the trails in VC and NVA uniforms.

Normally, the 281st Assault Helicopter Company was assigned in direct support. This was an extraordinary unit. Alert crews slept on the ships, ready to go pull a team out at a moment's notice. The gunships took off so heavily ammo-laden, they had to skip twice to get airborne and the slicks could inch down into a hole through which you'd swear a starling couldn't land.

There was also an Air Force FAC (Forward Air Control) team assigned, normally commanded by a USAF lieutenant colonel, and on one occasion there was a Marine Corps fighter wing assigned to the operational control of the Project, commanded by a major general. Probably the only instance in history of an Army major being in command of a Marine Corps major general.

In March of 1964 Major Allen, who was my friend and former commanding officer, asked me, in my capacity as Information Officer of the 5th Special Forces Group (Airborne) to accompany Delta on an operation in I Corps, the northernmost area of South Vietnam.

The mission was to do preliminary reconnaissance for a later major operation by Marine and Army units.

Delta set up a Forward Operational Base at Phu Bai, some tents and bunkers, a chopper pad, a zigzag trench, and some wire around the perimeter.

The idea was that I would see as much as I could and participate where possible. I couldn't go out with actual recon patrols—the teams were too tightly knit—but I could go with the reaction force, the 91st Airborne Ranger Battalion, and an attached Mobile Strike Force Company—the Mike Force—from Nha Trang. And I could fly in Chuck's Command and Control chopper on insertions and extractions. It was as much as an outsider could hope to see, and, in fact, before it was over I would apply and be accepted for transfer to Delta.

The first two stories in this series are rewrites of pieces I did for the *Green Beret*, the 5th Group's magazine. The first was originally written in the Delta FOB at Phu Bai; the second was written left-handed, in the 8th Field Hospital in Nha Trang. I've cleaned them and expanded a bit, and added some details that were classified at the time. The third story is an interview I did with Chuck for *Soldier of Fortune* in 1980.

# A Reconnaissance Mission

Just looking at them you could tell they were good.

Doc Betterton—Staff Sergeant Dale C. Betterton, a tall, skinny guy with a quiet manner, in glasses—stood on the platform in the briefing room at the Project Delta Forward Operational Base just outside Phu Bai. "We'll go in here," he tapped the map with his pointer, "and check out these areas. Primary mission is to locate enemy installations and personnel."

Taking all this in were five other team members—Betterton was the team leader. The other two Americans, Sergeant First Class Alberto Ortiz, Jr., who outranked Betterton, but was a new man on the Project and would not be given command of a team until he had a few patrols under his belt, and Sergeant John D. Anthony, watched the briefing.

The Vietnamese contingent consisted of First Lieutenant Ton That Hai, patrol leader, and Sergeants Nguyen Van Khan and Hoang Van Lieu.

They all listened with the same air of intense calm.

After listening to the brief-back in English, Lieutenant Hai repeated the information in Vietnamese.

In the rear of the room Major Chuck Allen, a massive crew-cut man, built like a pro football lineman, which he had been, leaned forward in his chair, one hand propped on his knee and the other under his chin. He did not appear to listen so much as to inhale the information, evaluating and storing it in a mind that tracked and controlled every detail of Delta.

Beside him his counterpart, Major Phan Van Huan, leaned back, his manner detached.

The chopper skimmed over the treetops, sun slowly extinguished by the mountains, throwing long shadows across the streambeds and valleys below.

*What is this now?* Doc thought. *Seventeen, maybe eighteen times in a year and a half. Every time, I'm still scared. That's good! A scared man is a careful man, and a careful man will live a long time. If I'm ever not afraid I'll go into some other line of work.*

Sitting in the left door of the helicopter, he followed the hills and valleys on his map. The wind whipped his tiger-striped trouser legs and floppy hat, hanging down his back on a homemade cord of parachute suspension line. A CAR-15 was slung over his shoulder by a triangular olive-drab bandage tied to the front sight and collapsible stock, which he would convert to a neckerchief when they reached the ground.

The seemingly endless maze of pockets on his tiger suit were jammed with notebooks, signaling devices, cigarettes, matches, and maps, all neatly folded into plastic bags. In his patrol harness were more signaling devices, a camera, and the ammunition he hoped not to use. On his back was a groundsheet, fourteen days' chow (long-range reconnaissance patrol rations, LRRPs) and some miscellaneous fruit cans.

The others were similarly equipped, plus two radios: one held by the Americans and one by the Vietnamese. Each was on a different frequency—to send the same data si-

multaneously to both the American and Vietnamese headquarters.

The ship started down, and he looked below into the dark
space in the trees that was their landing zone. The chopper
eased in and he was grateful again for the skill of the 281st
Aviation Company, Delta's own.

Trees rose on all sides; rotor blades snipping leaves
around the edges, the chopper inched its way down into the
hole. Master Sergeant Norman Doney, the reconnaissance
section leader, a handsome, soft-spoken, self-contained man
who would stay with the helicopter, rolled two ladders out
the door. Doc swung over the side.

His weight swung his feet straight out in front, he being
the bottom man on the rope ladder. His heavy gear dragged
as Doc started working his way down, all his weight on his
arms. Finally, his feet were below the ladder and he hung
by the bottom rung, eight feet above a bomb crater. He let
go. Ortiz dropped beside him from the other ladder and
they skipped sideways to get out of each other's way.

At a dead run they headed for the encircling jungle. Fifty
meters into the slapping, snagging brush they stopped. Doc
gulped air down fast to silence his panting.

Behind them the chopper sped away. The team lay listening under the brush and palms, fingers digging into wet
leaves and dirt while the dampness slowly permeated their
fatigues.

When Betterton gave the signal to rise, they slowly
crouched and stepped off single file into the jungle, walking
with their toes touching the ground first.

They made no more noise than wind sighing in the treetops. Tiger suits and camouflage greasepaint blended them
into their surroundings. If one of them sat perfectly still in
full view beside the trail, a man might walk by in broad
daylight and never see him.

They moved forward fifty meters, stopped, listened, and
moved on again. Using the last dregs of daylight the team

scanned for a thicket. Spotting a likely place, they glided back on their trail and sank to the earth in firing positions. No one came, so they crept into the thicket and slipped out of their packs.

Turning on the radio, Betterton whispered, "Voyager, this is Lobo, over."

In the handset a voice crackled back, "This Voyager, go."

Doc gave their positions in the same hoarse whisper and reported no contacts or sightings, while Hai did the same in Vietnamese. Then they wrapped up in their plastic groundsheets and fell asleep, each man touching at least one other. They still wore their pistol belts and harnesses. If they had to run they could manage without their packs, but not without water, ammo, and other gear on the harness.

With a rock gouging his shoulder blade and his hips digging into the ground, Doc slept fitfully. At 0330 the growl of heavy equipment and trucks snatched him from sleep. The enemy was building a road! Doc scribbled in his notebook.

At 0430 the patrol was up, creeping through the underbrush. Avoiding ridgelines and stream beds, they moved through the jungle on the slopes. Frequently they heard padding footsteps on the trails above, or the tonal ululations of Vietnamese conversation in the creeks below. There was no attempt at concealment on the enemy's part; he owned the territory and felt no need to hide from anything but airplanes. Again Doc scribbled, and spoke into the handset.

In the TOC (Tactical Operations Center) bunker Chuck Allen and Captain Bill Larabee, his operations officer, who looked like the social chairman of an especially bellicose Sigma Chi chapter, sat side by side at a big desk, plotting reports from their recon teams in the field. At a similar desk ten feet away Major Huan and Captain Ton That Luan did the same.

Seated across from Allen and Larrabee, Captain Richard Dundee, heavy and dark-complexioned, passed intelligence reports and summaries to major U.S. commands, while Lieutenant Truong Hoang Phi cranked out the same information to the Vietnamese Special Forces High Command.

No one on the patrol spoke a word except into the handset; they had worked so long together that no words were necessary, and silence was the rule. On the third day Hai gestured toward the trail above and made a grabbing motion with his hands. Doc, knowing he meant to try to capture a prisoner, nodded and they crept toward the path to wait.

Three North Vietnamese army regulars, all armed with AK-47's, came down the trail. They heard others chattering down the trail. No way. Betterton opened fire from five meters, and their "prisoners" shuddered backward as the slugs hit them, and they fell with blossoms of their own blood splattered across their midsections. The team broke off, one after the other, and dashed over the ridge and down the other side.

The next day Anthony almost walked headlong into another NVA soldier. They were both startled, but the kid was still staring wide-eyed when Anthony cut him down. They decided it was time to pull out. Betterton and Hai looked for LZs on their maps.

Allen saw it first. From his command-and-control ship, flying high over the operational area, he picked out the bright blue-white flash of a signaling mirror and spoke into his radio. Gunships, easy to spot by their red tail markings, assumed a clockwise orbit over the LZ, either firing at targets of opportunity or just keeping Charlie's head down. The air was filled with the whoooosh-CRACK of rockets and the gruff belch of miniguns.

Flying above, monitoring all conversation between his ship, the gunships, the TOC and the recon team on the ground, Allen could see it all like a Parker Bros. game. At his command the first recovery ship hopped over a ridgeline and jockeyed down into the hole.

Doc Betterton put the mirror back into his ammo pouch. The others fanned out in firing positions around him. The incoming recovery ship hovered a hundred feet over them in the trees. Although Doc couldn't see Doney in the ship, he knew who it was.

Three sandbags dragged the heavy, six-foot looped straps of the McGuire rig, escape for three men, down through the trees. Doc waved Ortiz and the two Vietnamese sergeants in, and they grabbed the straps, whipping and writhing in the rotor wash. Each of them sat in one loop and hooked his right wrist in a cuff that slid down tight to prevent falling from the rig, even if wounded, on the way out.

The chopper struggled to go straight up without dragging the men through the trees. This was the period of maximum danger—maximum exposure of the helicopter and maximum exposure for the men. They cleared the trees and were gone.

The next ship edged into position and the straps came down again. Doc, the heaviest of the three, jumped into the middle seat as the others settled next to him. The chopper eased upward and they rose through the trees, branches slapping at their faces and hands.

Then they were clear of the treetops and the ropes streamed to the rear as the chopper surged forward, heading for a safe spot to land and take the men inside. No matter how many times he did it, Doc never got completely used to whipping through the air at the end of a rope, at a thousand feet.

# With the Mike Force

The day after Betterton's team came out, the Mike Force went in. Betterton, Dundee the Delta Intelligence officer, and I went along as well, Doc because he knew the ground, and Dundee to personally collect intelligence. The rest of us were there to see that he lived to get it. The 281st had knocked out an entire NVA truck convoy two weeks before, and Chuck wanted Dundee to photograph their bumper markings to identify the unit.

The Rangers had been in right after to perform the same mission, but hadn't been able to do it. The NVA were so thick in that area that when one of them came upon the Rangers and didn't see the Americans with them he assumed they were another NVA unit. He walked up to one of them and asked in Vietnamese, "What outfit are you guys with?"

"You'll have to ask the lieutenant," the Ranger replied.

The NVA, now starting to feel a little nervous, stepped up to the ARVN Ranger *Thieu Uy*, and asked, "Uh, Comrade Lieutenant, what—"

"Ninety-first Airborne Ranger Battalion," the lieutenant replied, and stitched him right up the middle with his M16. This was a costly gesture, since one of their missions was to capture a prisoner, and now their mission was blown. So they came out and we went in.

Doc Betterton led the Mike Force over the ground his recon had covered. The Mike Force wore helmets, but Doc wore his recon boonie hat; the Mike Force stepped right out— you can't move a hundred guys in total silence—and Doc was used to moving around out here on tiptoe; the Mike Force moved on the trails, and recon *never* moves on trails. He didn't look very happy.

Our first contact was so light it was scarcely worth reporting. We were taking a break when an NVA came up the main trail and was surprised to see a stocky blond American, SP-5 Sammy Coutts, leaning against a tree.

A month before in downtown Nha Trang, on the first day of the Tet Offensive, I'd seen Coutts dash into the middle of a street under heavy fire to drag a young Vietnamese girl to safety. That had been my first acquaintance with this company, but I'd been around them some since, though not in combat. The 7th MSF company were mainly Cham, a coastal fishing people, Muslims.

The Charlie who had spotted Coutts scurried away and came back with his buddies a few minutes later. By that time we were moving again and Coutts was down the trail. They hit the tail of the column. The 4th platoon opened up, and there followed one of those brief, inconclusive firefights in which neither side gives or takes much of anything.

The terrain was rough and densely wooded, but not as much as most of the Highlands. These were big hills, not mountains, and the woods no worse than many in Georgia. It was beautiful country.

A little later, during the lunch break, a Mike Force perimeter guard challenged a rustling noise in the bushes. The challenge was answered by a burst of AK-47 fire, killing the guard.

Sergeant First Class Ross Potter, a darkly handsome karate black belt, was in command of the Mike Force Company. He led the company off the trail and uphill, quickly,
tripping over commo wire on the ground—commo wire?
—through the woods to a place where the trees were fairly
sparse. A HU-1D helicopter from the 281st came in to
winch the body out. The clearing wasn't as wide as the
rotor disc of the aircraft.

The pilot inched his chopper down through the trees,
straight in until a limb got in his way, backed or slipped
sideways around it, down three feet, over two, down four,
over three. Finally they lowered their winch and picked up
the small poncho-wrapped body, still tied to a one-pole litter. Then they inched that chopper back out again the same
way.

We reported the commo wire on our first scheduled contact the next morning. Chuck, or somebody in Saigon, decided we needed to tap it, and, since Delta wasn't equipped
for that, a team from Command and Control FOB 1 at Phu
Bai was choppered in. The C & C teams had a mission
similar to Delta's, except they generally performed it in
Laos or North Vietnam. They had a horrendous casualty
rate, rumored to be two hundred percent a year, compared
to Delta's fifty.

They barreled out of a 281st slick, and looked at us with
raccoon eyes. The Americans with them were hard boys,
but nothing special for Special Forces. But their indidge
were fascinating. The Vietnamese leader was an ARVN
warrant officer, very calm and competent. The rest of the
team were crazy people; the Americans were on a one-year
tour, but this was the Viets' *life*. One had sunken cheeks
and fierce eyes; he wore a ring in his ear, an all-black bush
hat, blocked like Clint Eastwood's, and black gloves which
he constantly smoothed back. Another looked like Dopey
of the Seven Dwarfs, except that he was badly pockmarked

and giggled constantly. The last looked like a zombie, and his eyes were windows to a dead zone.

They didn't pick up anything useful off the wire, and seemed to think the job was a joke—a Lennie Bruce joke, but a joke. They were with us for the rest of the mission, and their attitude seemed to be . . . well, hey, everybody's got to be someplace.

That night we heard the same trucks grinding uphill that the recon team had heard earlier. The following morning we checked the road; there were few signs that any activity had taken place the night before. Charlie did a good job covering his tracks.

After two firefights the day before the company stuck to the hillsides, going over the ridgelines only when they had to maintain the patrol's route. After a full day's march with no contact and no sightings, when it was about time to hang it up for the day, we stumbled across a couple of cases of twenty-three-millimeter ammunition, the kind that goes with a very large Russian antiaircraft machine-gun. The ammo looked as though it was being carried across a stream when Charles dropped it during an air strike. The ammo lay on the trail a few feet off the creek bottom. The crates had been broken open and a few rounds removed.

Dundee took pictures of the cache. Then the company headed down a small bank and into a creek. There was a quick chatter of gunfire and the point went down. Cordite smoke poured out of the creek bottom as the Cham returned fire. It was a platoon, probably back for more ammo. The Cham took out six Charlies.

Then another group came in from the other side. Hearing a lot of gunfire, they came better prepared.

What with being caught in a crossfire, and darkness coming on fast, we got the hell out of there, not in very good order, no panic, but not exactly a perfect formation either. We just got the fuck out.

The night was dark. We slept clinging to the side of a hill like moss.

Early the next morning the Cham hacked out a landing zone with machetes and evaced their dead and wounded. The company moved cautiously down the trail to check out the ammo boxes again.

Captain Dundee had just gotten the last of his pictures when three more Cong showed up and the firefight was on again. The Cham made short work of them and we moved out.

On the next break Potter said, "I think I'll have to revise my estimate of enemy strength in this area up from one to two companies."

"Yeah," replied Doc Betterton. "Either that or a highly mobile squad."

We moved out again. Only, this time we had picked up a tail. Every time we stopped or started, the familiar signal shot ring out, alerting the entire neighborhood.

When we crossed a little finger of the ridgeline, we ran into a series of large ammo caches. They were dug into cubical pits in the ground, about eight feet on a side, braced with bamboo so they wouldn't cave in. They were well made. Potter had an order passed to the 4th Platoon. As the platoon, advised by Staff Sergeant Ken Roberts, passed the caches, they rigged them with time fuses. Five minutes after the 4th Platoon moved through, the first cache blew, destroying a sizable portion of the ammunition and leaving the remainder to cook off. It continued exploding for the rest of the afternoon and long into the evening.

Around the middle of the afternoon the most satisfactory sounds came, as Charlie's backtracking team got into a firefight with their own exploding ammunition.

We came out on the two-lane dirt road that Charles had been building through the dense woods, down in the flats between hills. We wanted to get to an LZ and get out, and that road was the quickest way. It was an eerie feeling to be walking down that road like Stateside troops coming back from an exercise. I heard NVA a few meters back in the woods, chattering. It was normal conversation; they weren't aware of us at all, just hauling wood, making fires, cleaning weapons, smoking pot.

Delta's forward air controller droned overhead, flying cover, a little boom-tail aircraft with fore and aft propellers, the OV1.

Dug into the sides of the hills we walked past were one- and two-man foxholes, some dug in an L-shape, probably for crew-served weapons, rockets, and machine guns.

The company came upon the nine Russian trucks the 281st gunships had knocked out the week before. They lay strewn on the road, burned and gutted. Dundee took intelligence photos of the trucks and the bumper markings, and I snapped Dundee for the Group magazine.

We moved down the road again for about half a klick to a good LZ. The Cham set up a perimeter and waited for the choppers. The longer we waited the more NVA came to get in on the act. We were completely surrounded on and around a big bare red-dirt clearing, dotted with four or five B-52 bomb craters. The firefight continued sporadically for about an hour and a half, enemy strength continuing to build as we waited. Air cover was called in to keep the tightening noose of NVA off until slicks from the 281st could get us out.

F-105's made run after run, huge aircraft making that cracking jet roar, dropping five-hundred pound high-drag bombs into the jungle so close that smoking chunks of jagged steel bounced into our holes. Then we heard the familiar sound of approaching helicopters.

When we got back Dundee's photos didn't come out, so Delta confiscated all of mine.

Two days later I went back into the same LZ with a company from the Ranger battalion. We went in in two lifts, and by the time the second came we were surrounded again. We were pinned onto the LZ all night with six choppers down and thirty percent casualties, me among them.

The next day we fought our way to another LZ and got out. That was my last operation; I retired because of wounds. Although I was never on their roster, I am proud that Delta counts me among their alumni.

# The Ether Zone

*Project Delta comes from the ether zone of military excellence.*

—LIEUTENANT GENERAL ROBERT CUSHMAN, USMC

Lieutenant Colonel Charles A. Allen, former commander of SF Det B-52 (Project Delta), was a huge man, weighing more than 250 pounds, strong as a bull. He differed considerably from the stereotyped career officer. To begin with, he was a draftee.

He wasn't exactly dodging the draft; he was just a young man drifting around after leaving school, having a good time, playing a little semipro football here, bouncing in bars there.

One day, when he was bouncing in a bar in Florida, a gentleman from the government showed up and asked if he'd gotten much mail lately. The man wasn't from the quality-control division of the Post Office; he was from the FBI, and the letter he was referring to began, *Greetings . . .*

So off Allen went. He never looked back. His military career encountered a hitch when he coldcocked the chief of staff of the 82nd Airborne Division in the commanding general's office. They were putting the pressure on him to play football, but he insisted that he was in the Army to soldier. After making this point several times, he decided to leave; the colonel showed poor judgment in placing his hand on Allen's chest to restrain him. Not a good move.

That kept him a captain for twelve years. If he hadn't done that, he probably would have retired a full colonel. If he had kept his hands to himself and also gone to college, he probably would have retired a general. As it is, all he did was command in combat a unit good enough to take its place in legend alongside the Knights of the Round Table and Robin Hood's Merry Men.

We met late in the evening at his print shop, amid layouts of city magazines and weekly newspapers. But those displayed on the walls were covers for *The Drop*, the magazine of the Special Forces Association. Allen has always worked late hours, and he attacked civilian life with the same drive and dedication he had brought to war. As always, there was a big pot of coffee, and we started talking about the Project.

"I used to love hanging around with you guys," I said, "because everybody down there seemed to know exactly what he was doing. It was the greatest collection of brains, class, and talent I ever saw in one place at one time."

Allen took a sip of coffee and smiled. "Well, nobody got assigned to Delta; they were assigned for interview. And it was maybe an unfair screening process we went through. My God, by the time a man reported to me for interview, he'd been screened five or six times—within Delta.

"And then if I accepted the guy into the unit, recon would screen him. And I don't mean they'd talk to him for twenty minutes. He'd go over and stay with them for three, four, or five days, and at the end of that time, if they thought he might be a good Joe, they'd say, 'Okay, sir, we'd like to have him.' That's after I, the CO, had said, 'Hey, I wanna take this guy and put him in recon.'

"And if they didn't want him I'd back them up.

"You remember Doc Simpson, my recon platoon leader? I had a lot of faith in Doc, and if he said, 'Everybody else thinks this guy is good, but I really don't think he's gonna make it,' he wouldn't take him. If I thought he was good, I'd assign him somewhere else in Delta. I'd send him over to the Rangers or put him in Roadrunners or something like that."

I lifted an eyebrow. "Was recon pretty much the elite within the elite within the elite?"

Allen nodded. "Yeah. It was almost the reason for Delta's existence."

"I didn't hang out with those guys too much," I admitted. "They knew I was going to write them up, and a lot of them didn't want that."

"Well," Allen replied, "you know, to go out and be dropped into an area that someone has selected as the hottest he can put you into is bad enough by itself, but then to have to live through whatever the outcome is of your time on the ground and get out successfully and say, 'Hey, I've got a recon mission under my belt, and it was a hot one,' that's something to be proud of. It was not like the Korean War, going on a patrol overnight with thirty-five other guys and maybe you make contact and maybe not. It was a whole lot different, because you were completely cut off and isolated from everything, from any type of support, particularly during the hours of darkness. Because then your support just wasn't there.

"So the fact that you had a successful one under your belt made you one of the boys. And the more you got, the prouder you became. The most successful and best people were a real weird breed. They were loners usually, though among themselves they'd be very clannish. But around someone who had never been on a recon patrol, they were complete loners, almost to the point of having a complex about it."

"Yeah," I said, "Nobody—because I asked—nobody let a straphanger go on recon, because if there'd have been one, I'd have been him."

"Yeah,"—he nodded earnestly—"you can't do it. You just can't. There're too many immediate action drills and procedures that they know from working closely together. Just the wink of an eye, or maybe two winks, means to do something; a straphanger out there would be completely lost. The first thing you know, you're givin' him on-the-job training in the field."

I asked if Delta had used the Recondo School, the school for long-range recon in Nha Trang, to train their people. No, their training was different.

"How was it different?" I asked.

"Well, for one thing, in Delta, if you got assigned and were okayed to go to recon, then those were the people you trained with."

"Did the teams have control over their own training?" I asked.

"No, it was closely monitored by my staff. When we had training, we had training; there was no leeway in it. It was very disciplined, and it followed lesson plans, and all the lesson plans were revised to include subjects that were learned in the field from previous recon experience.

"And when they finished, the guys on the team all knew the same thing. If a new man joined the team and he had to be trained then they all went through it with him, whether they had been through it ten times or one time, which means that the recipient of the training was getting the advantage of that training plus the experience of the other guys in the team who had had that training and put it to use in the field."

"So instead of one instructor for ten guys, it worked the other way."

"Right! Everybody was working to train that one man, but they also were going through it themselves. That's the concept we used and it seemed to work okay."

Then we got into operational aspects.

"This is what I considered a perfect recon team mission," Allen said. He started to grin. His grin is kind of lopsided; he has a chipped tooth and his eyes glitter. "We had information that NVA were moving down. We had a pretty hot area where we had just pulled that Blackjack Operation—a thirty-day mobile guerrilla-force operation in NVA territory—by the II Corps Mike Force.

"You remember Clyde Sincere, the first II Corps Mike Force commander? He had that operation that caught a short bomb and his Montagnard troops got spooked—bad Buddha. They turned on the Americans and we had to pull 'em out.

"There was no question that there were a lot of people out there in the bushes. So we put in a recon team with three Americans and four Vietnamese."

"Why three Americans—didn't you usually use two?"

"Well," he replied, "we liked to use three. Using two Americans is tough because if one got hit we only had one to carry him out. We couldn't, in all cases, expect that kind of cooperation out of our brothers, the Vietnamese. They'd take care of themselves, but if an American got hit, they wouldn't worry too much about it. With the three-man team, if one guy got hit, you'd have two Americans to care for him and carry him out.

"So we picked an area that we knew was a natural route—by route I mean sloping ground: not open territory, but along a stream bed or an old road or something. It was part of what everybody called the Ho Chi Minh Trail, which was probably fifty miles wide. People think it was a little concrete walkway through the woods.

"We picked this area because intelligence indicated that there were good-sized units coming in there. I had some that specifically pinpointed that area. We used the normal team procedure: went in by helicopter at last light, and put the team in. They moved a hundred yards or so that night, into a deep bamboo thicket, and dug in to bed down for the night.

"At first light the team leader called in and gave us this location so we knew exactly where he was. And about that time he heard a lot of voices. He sent one of the guys to peek out of this bamboo grove and, there, not a hundred yards away, across this little stream and under the trees, was what looked to be a battalion, weapons all neatly stacked, and they're getting up and starting their little fires to cook their rice.

"And the next thing you knew there was normal military activity taking place. The first sergeant got out in front and started yelling, kicking ass, and taking names.

"By this time my team leader was about to wet his pants; this is a storybook situation, and with this particular operation everything right that could happen happened. He got back to the TOC [Tactical Operation Center] radio relay. We put in an air request right away. It just so happened there was a flight of 105's coming back from up north on a Rolling Thunder mission. They'd hit bad weather up there at first light, so they couldn't expend. They were coming back hot. They had full loads on.

"We put a request in. They were turned over to us immediately. It was really too quick even to get a FAC (Forward Air Controller) out there. In the meantime the battalion started taking their jackets off and lining up in a PT formation; dress right, cover down, you know.

"And then, by God, they started doing exercises, regular physical training exercises. Well, what happened is that the team leader was given instructions to let his smoke go, and book it. And as I say, everything happened—timing on it couldn't have been better planned if a genius had done it. They threw the smoke, did a one-eighty, and started making it back. And about the time the smoke popped, here came the jets in on short final, the smoke coming up through the trees.

"The team's first report said there was some scurrying around over there; jets came in at treetop level and salvoed-

dropped everything they had. The entire PT formation was engulfed in napalm and five hundred pounders. The team did not go back over to do a bomb-damage assessment. We sent in the Nung [members of a tribe of hereditary Chinese mercenaries] platoon."

"That was your bomb-damage assessment platoon?"

"Yeah, that was the BDA team, because I always felt that if I had a Nung platoon out there, they would do what they were told by their American leaders—if they were separated on the ground and gave any intelligence at all back to the adviser, we could believe what they said.

"And, of course, we commanded the Nungs. We did not command the ARVN. We were advisers to them. But the Nungs—we paid 'em, we fed 'em, we commanded 'em. They were just like another troop. So we sent the BDA platoon back in later that afternoon, after we got the team out. That team was on the ground probably fourteen or fifteen hours at the most. In the morning they were probably on the ground and working for an hour.

"We have no way of knowing how many we cooked, but indications were that hundreds were killed. It's a fluke, I guess—that things fell together and that there happened to be a flight of Tac Air available right at the moment we asked for it, and that the request was approved immediately. The flight came in right as the smoke popped, and we were right on target.

"When we sent the Nungs back in, we found burnt weapons and uniforms. We didn't find many bodies—a lot of them had been taken. We didn't think it was wise to go searching the whole valley for them. But we did find indications of a lot of deaths: arms hanging in trees and that kind of stuff.

"That was one of our main missions: to find something and bring smoke in on 'em, because we always operated out of artillery range, except when the Cav had their eight-inchers out there."

I poured myself another cup and said, "That was the perfect recon, but it wasn't always like that. I remember that when the Project started, the Americans didn't even go out. Let's see. The Project existed for about six years, from '64 to what—'70, '71?

"Yeah," Allen replied, "for a long time it was just a base for training Vietnamese in certain operations. It wasn't an operational unit. It was the old stigma of having the Vietnamese in command, not being able to fly the American flag in the compound, being the adviser and all that stuff.

"The sophistication I talked about before, that we built into it, came from the fact that I required the 281st [Assault Helicopter Company] to be in direct support and actually attached to us. We made them part of the Project, you know. They wore tiger suits and they wore the Delta triangles. We required that the Air Force guys move down there and be part of the unit: get to know the guys and live with us, right in the compound. We had Marines in there, too—the strategic communications group that ran the scramblers and stuff between us and III MAF were attached to us and lived with us. Some of those Marines were with Project Delta for nine months. We required that they be part of the unit. They trained with the unit; everybody did. It was one unit, not just a conglomeration of attached units.

"And, as such, we actually commanded the unit—before, all operations had to be commanded and okayed by the Vietnamese counterpart, which would plan an operation to get the least contact. When we were holding the hammer there, we controlled everything that ran the operation: money for the compound, gas for the trucks—'Use my jeep, *Thieu Ta*, if you want to go out tonight'—ammunition, air strikes, air support. We had a hammer so we could say if we want to fly the American flag we will fly it. We plan an operation, and if you want to come along you can.

"In fact, during my tenure there we did run one or two operations where we left the Vietnamese in the compound.

We caught all kinds of hell about it, though."

"But the one time we did that, it was just a matter of survival. It was the Tet offensive. I sent my teams over to Nha Trang to get some people out of trouble; they got caught in some houses over there, so we sent some men over to get them to bring our own people home, y'know?"

"You guys had the plushest setup: your garrison facilities there, your compound, that NCO club, all that stuff you had going in there when I left. You know you had that big, padded Delta-shaped bar in the NCO club, and you had your rock garden in the officers' club, and the fountains and the paintings . . ."

Allen smiled at the memory. If Delta had lived a Spartan existence in the field, its garrison facilities had been *la dolce vita*. "I would hate to say how much money went into that compound. A lot of it, of course, was material that was procured down at Cam Ranh Bay. We had a couple of NCOs who'd go down there and take paint and stencils with them and walk into the truck park where all the new trucks were. They'd stencil the bumper numbers on the truck and get in it and drive home, but only after they'd taken it to some other depot and filled it with air-conditioners, cement, tin roofing, or whatever we needed. The stuff was readily available. It was there for the asking, so to speak, so we took advantage of it."

"The hot rumor when I left was that you were going to build yourselves an Olympic-size swimming pool so you wouldn't have to go the two miles to the beach for scuba and small-boat training. Did you ever get it built?"

Allen leaned forward. "Well, we had all the equipment—cement, steel reinforcing bars, and we'd purchased the diving board in Hong Kong. We had everything we needed to put the pool in, including the tile. We had the hole dug right out behind the mess hall. Then somebody thought that was going a little too far in a war zone, so we had to trade off what we had.

"The sad thing about it all was that the day after the Project closed and they turned it over to the Vietnamese, they came through and ripped it apart, pulled the plumbing out of the walls—ruined it in one day. They tore the buildings down, sold the lumber, the tin and everything. About the only thing that I salvaged out of it was—do you remember the brass plaque on the pole in the officers' club: it said, THE ETHER ZONE, BUILT BY THE OFFICERS OF PROJECT DELTA, and listed them all? That was mysteriously sent to me in a package about five years ago. I really don't know who got it or how, but it showed up in my mailbox one day with a note that said, *Bruiser, if anybody should have this, you should.* Signed *A Friend.* I have it at home in my bar.

"Our concept required that everybody give in the field. It was easy to say, 'Give me your all,' because when we got back to camp it was 'Don't give me anything. Take it easy; enjoy yourself. Have fun today, because tomorrow you're going back at it again.' I think a lot of them lived like it was their last day on earth. They had parties—we provided the best in food, the best in entertainment. We had the best morale of anybody around anywhere. . . ."

"That's right," I agreed. "Your guys were superstars, the best individual soldiers in Vietnam."

"They knew it too."

"When you think about it, it was really a super military organization. There you were, a major, and you had an American Air Force lieutenant colonel and a Vietnamese lieutenant colonel working for you."

Allen chuckled. "Hangin' around anyway."

"At one time you even had a Marine Corps major general working for you."

"Yeah," Allen replied. "Jesus, that was surprising. General Anderson. He reported in and said, 'Major, I'm op-con to you and you do what you want with me. I'm here to help you. General Cushman said to give you every bit of support we've got. So you have the 1st Marine Air Wing at your disposal.' He said it kind of jokingly, but he played the game. General Anderson moved right into the TOC with us and stayed there about two days. He slept and ate with us; he was one of the boys, and one hell of a help. Because, my God, we must have used a hundred-and-some odd sorties during that operation."

We broke it up about ten-thirty that night. Allen's wife had called to say that the war was over and his supper was waiting.

The next morning he picked me up in his new car. He is the only man I know who makes a Mark IV look like a Toyota. We started talking about awards and decorations and, in illustrating a point about impact awards, Allen told me one of the few combat stories that has raised the hair on the back of my neck.

"Coffey? You remember Ed Coffey, coffee-colored Coffey?"

"Yeah, I think so. He was a kind of skinny, good-looking guy, and he really was coffee-with-cream colored?"

"Weapons man. He was with me at Khe Sanh." Allen commanded the first USAF A Team at Khe Sanh in 1963. "He was with me several places, including here at Bragg.

"Coffey was on the ground with a Ranger Company; he was a Ranger adviser. They got into all kinds of hell; they probably got inside of two or three battalions. They had gone up a long L-shaped ridge and made contact and then were gonna come down the remainder of this ridge into low ground where we could pick 'em up, to get them out of there. And they ran into more.

"So we started putting air strikes in, which were very effective, because the lower portions of both sides were manioc fields, and you could see them running around there, all over the place.

"We put in God knows how many flights—cleaned off the bottom portion of this ridge and the spine and the entire top portion. In the meantime Coffey and his crew cleared an LZ on a little saddle, and then we started taking them out. We probably had everybody out except fifteen or twenty people.

"And do you remember Herb Siugzda? On Okinawa he was a real wild cook; he was Lithuanian or something like that. He came to Delta as a cook, but ended up later in recon. He got wounded two or three times, pretty badly—jumped out of a chopper one time, right onto a pungi, one of the big ones, that came up through his nuts and into his stomach. They put him on a hospital ship for three months, and he came back to Delta and begged me to let him go back out on patrol.

"So we got him retrained, and goddamn, he wasn't on the ground five minutes before he caught one right in the middle of the chest. He was on the ground altogether twenty minutes. After he got back from that one, he was medevacked home.

"Anyway, we'd got 'em down to probably fifteen or twenty people on the ground; Coffey and Siugzda and the little guy who helped you with Link. You remember?"

I remembered well enough. We had tried and failed to save Link's life, and in the process the "little guy" and I were both badly wounded. "Merriman?"

"Yeah, Merriman. Siugzda was on the radio and Merriman was there with them. A chopper came in to pick up the next-to-the-last load. Just before it came in, Coffey got hit in the back of the neck with an AK round. It tore his jaw completely off—everything was gone, just a big gaping hole here." Chuck made a motion with his hand that swept his lower jaw away.

"The ship came in and settled down. Then, about the time the troops were loading into the ship, Charlie stood up about two hundred yards away with an AK leveled down on the pilot, but before he could fire, Coffey saw him. Coffey was all field packs and dressings around his head and everything, but he grabbed his weapon and sat up and shot the guy dead.

"Okay, that ship got out. Every ship that went in and came out of that LZ that day came out with holes in it—many holes. We lost two or three of them that day. We got the crews all out, but we lost the ships.

"I think that was the last slick we had available, so we had to wait for a couple more to come back before we could get the first crew out. All this time we had gunships working the perimeters of the LZ, and of course we had air strikes going in as they became available, and FACs to direct them in. All this time Coffey is directing air strikes, by pad.

"And Siugzda was talking to me. I was concerned about Coffey, because we'd been close. Needless to say, we didn't get any ships back. The LZ started getting a lot hotter and there were only about four or five of them left on the ground. So we went in and picked them up on the C-and-C ship. Took a couple holes in it as I recall."

Allen looked pained, telling me this part; he didn't want himself as hero. He wanted to tell me how great his guys were, so I mentally multiplied his "couple holes" by a factor of about thirty. "It was a normal thing that happens. If it doesn't hit anybody, fine. It's no big thing." He shrugged.

Sure, Chuck.

"Well, we got Coffey in and back over to Da Nang to the hospital. This was when I learned about him shooting that NVA. So I told him I was awarding him an interim Silver Star on the spot. And I told him that I would personally guarantee that he got that or higher. We landed on the chopper pad at the hospital in Da Nang.

"The doctor on the C team there was a very dedicated Green Beret doctor. They got Coffey onto a stretcher, but by the time they got him into the room he was dead.

"I think he may have died in the chopper, lying across my lap.

"That was one time I made an award that I really wasn't authorized to.

"I subsequently found out, within twenty minutes or so, that when they checked Coffey, they found he'd been shot in the back: It went directly through the heart and came out the front. There was a hole in his chest you could put your fist in. But only the guys on the ground had noticed that; because it looked like the blood and stuff from his chin had dripped down. The doctor told me he just couldn't understand or explain how in the world Coffey could have lived as long as he did.

"And apparently this shot through the heart was from the same burst as the one that hit him in the neck and took his jaw off, because there were no other times he could have been hit."

That was when the hair raised on the back of my neck. Because that doctor was right—there was no physical way the man could have survived; he did it on spirit. General Cushman called it the Ether Zone, but he could have just as well said the Twilight Zone.

"We subsequently put Coffey in for the Medal of Honor, because the fact was that he'd taken two rounds, either one of which was a fatal wound. I think the final award that he got was the DSC, posthumous DSC. We resubmitted for consideration, but it never came.

"How about unit awards?"

"The Marines were fairly instrumental in giving Delta some credit that was due."

"What all did you get?"

"We got two Presidential units, an Army meritorious, the Army valorous unit award, and the Navy valorous unit award, a Marine-initiated thing. We got the Vietnamese unit award, Cross of Gallantry with palm. We got two of those, and whatever else. I don't know. There were a bunch of them. They were all earned, I guess."

"I would say so."

"I think Delta was probably one of the most decorated units in Vietnam, as opposed to all the unit decorations the 1st Cav Division got."

"Yeah, but Delta wasn't comparable to anything else; it was just itself," I said. "You can't say it was a battalion-size unit. It doesn't really relate to the Special Forces team concept."

"The problem with being completely different is that sometimes decisions about deployment are made by staff people who can't think past the end of their SOP. And Delta ran into problems like that on more than one occasion.

"Just before I came home, they were having trouble in Saigon. The NVA took over the racetrack and were getting into downtown Saigon at night.

"This was much later than Tet. It's that other campaign they conducted down there. Someone at 5th Group got the idea that recon teams would be great in house-to-house fighting.

"Say . . . what?"

"You heard me right. And Ken Nauman went down as task force commander because he was going to be the XO of Delta. Bob Mays was to be commander. He took over from me.

"They went down and camped at the racetrack outside of Saigon, and proceeded to have five or six Vietnamese teams wasted immediately. It was really sad. Fact is, they lost three or four Americans in that operation down there. It was really bad. I sat there in our compound for four or five days waiting for our flight, reading the Op reports at night. And goddamn, I just cried. I couldn't believe it. They lost these Americans in the first three or four days down there. It was a damn shame.

"I don't know who made the decision. . . . It was just a misuse. I don't know how long they stayed there. I went home brokenhearted, you know."

He grinned sardonically when he said it, the old Chuck Allen grin. He didn't look brokenhearted; he looked like a man who has accomplished his mission. He looked triumphant, as always.

# JUMPERS

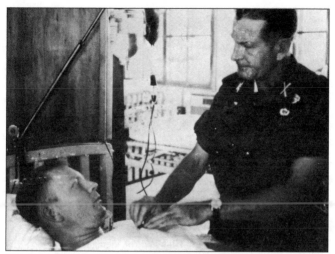

Col. John Spears, CO of the 5th Special Forces Group (Airborne), presents Morris with Purple Hearts numbers two and three.

Capt. Crews McCulloch with dead water buffalo on patrol in Phu Bon Province.

View from a helicopter over the Highlands of Vietnam. (*Courtesy of Larry Dring*)

Paratrooper jump.
(*Courtesy of Larry Dring*)

Special Forces trooper fires the M1 on the range. (*Courtesy of Larry Dring*)

Lt. Larry Dring spots for the .30 caliber machine gun.

Helicopter attempts to land at a fire base while under attack. (*Courtesy of Larry Dring*)

Morris on the drop zone in Thailand, after having parachuted from a barrage balloon in 1982.

Capt. Larry O'Neill heads down an alley during city fighting in Nha Trang. Morris with rifle and hand-held camera on right.

Capt. J. Scottt Gantt calls in helicopter gunships on an NVA-held neighborhood in Nha Trang during Tet 1968.

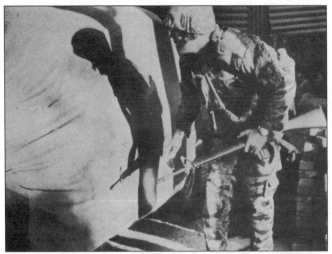

Nha Trang, Tet 1968. By the end of the day, that car looked like Swiss cheese.

Special Forces trooper shows Cambodian female soldier how to fire the mortar. *(Courtesy of Larry Dring)*

Rigger check prior to jump.

Larry Dring in the jungle with a captured NVA flag. *(Courtesy of Larry Dring)*

Special Forces trooper fires the pistol on the range in Pleiku.
*(Courtesy of Larry Dring)*

# Airborne—All the Way

My first jump story was written in 1962, in the offices of *Pacific Stars and Stripes* on Okinawa. As information officer of the 1st Special Forces Group (Airborne) I dropped in one day to see Sid White, the bureau chief, and while there asked if he might like a Sunday feature on a night drop in Korea. He said he would and I sat down in front of a typewriter and wrote it in about an hour. When I started putting this collection together I hadn't read it in almost thirty years.

I've made around a hundred and fifty jumps since, and was wistfully amused at my own gee-whiz attitude in the story. Back then all you had to do was say "parachute" and I started to breathe faster.

When I went airborne we thought the day of the mass drop was over, but we knew one of the main values of parachuting was that it taught a young soldier to perform simple mechanical tasks while scared shitless. That, after all, is the challenge in combat, and there is no better psychological preparation for it than parachuting.

In addition to the gee-whiz attitude there was also a gung-ho unabashedly patriotic spirit. After having spent the past twenty years trying to explain to my fellow Americans that I am not an ax murderer, it was surprising and saddening to remember the time when we thought risking our lives for our country was heroic, and expected to be perceived that way by the people we were doing it for.

The other three stories appeared respectively in *Soldier of Fortune, Esquire*, and *EAGLE*.

It's been twenty-eight years now since the first one, and it might be instructive to mention what's happened to the people in these stories. George Lee, who was ahead of me in the stick on that night drop, was killed in Vietnam when his aircraft was shot down on an aerial recon.

Captain Crews McCulloch, my CO in "Chinese Fire Drill," resigned his commission after that tour. In 1964, before the first U.S. troop units were deployed, he said to me, "Jim, we are going to lose this war, and there is nothing you or I can do about it. I don't want to stick around to see it." Crews was a Regular Army captain on the five percent list for major and on orders for Command and General Staff School when he resigned.

If you've been in the army you know that means he was destined to be a general, and no one who knew him expected him to retire with fewer than three stars.

He's been a successful businessman, an unsuccessful candidate for Congress, a good husband, and the father of two great daughters. Through it all he continued to teach Sunday School.

I believed him about the war, but I wanted to see it through, to write the great Vietnam War novel.

Cowboy is dead, killed in a Montagnard intermural squabble in 1968. Khue is dead, I think, simply because all of the 'Yards who fought with us are dead, either killed outright by the Vietnamese when they took over, or killed fighting with the Montagnard resistance after. Only 220 out of all those tens of thousands made it to the States, and Le Van Khue was not among them.

Bill Foody is now a surgeon and a colonel in the Air Force in San Antonio. Ed Thomas retired as a sergeant major. The Reeds continued to do missionary work in the Philippines after they left Vietnam. I have heard they are now settled in the States.

Sergeant Brown from "Meet Me in the Middle of the Air" was killed on a recon into Laos with CCN. Ed Rybat retired as a colonel, after having commanded CCN and later a military training team to Liberia during the revolution there. I have lost track of everybody else.

The original plan for this collection was that the stories be about heroes I have known, but these jump stories are all first person. To get them right I had to get inside the jumper's head and mine was the only head available. Once, on one of those night drops in Korea, the jumper behind Father Kovacic, our rangy Catholic chaplain, said, "Well, Father, I guess you and God will be going out the door in a minute."

"No, son," replied the priest, "He says good-bye in the door and meets you on the ground, but this is one thing you've got to do by yourself."

# Night Drop

There is no tension in the face of your fellow jumpers, but you know it is there. No tension shows in your own face, either, but you can feel it. This is a peculiar form of fear, and easy to fight because you know there is no rational reason for it.

Parachuting is a relatively safe way to make a living. The equipment is good; the Air Force is good, and, looking around, you know the jumpers are good. They are old troopers from the 1st Special Forces Group on Okinawa. Most of them have been jumping for years.

So, rationally, there is no reason to be afraid. True, there is a slight risk of breaking a leg, and sprains are common.

You know for a fact this will be a hard fall. It is on the Han River #2 Drop Zone, and in the summer the sand is as soft as a bowl of mush. But it is winter now, and the DZ is frozen into glazed granite and there will be no soft landings tonight. In all probability there will be sprains, but nothing broken. Knock wood.

But the fear is still there, building. Not a rational fear, but man's oldest fear, fear of falling. So you can fight it and overcome it. But never will it go away completely. Not in a thousand jumps, not in a million, and certainly not in the paltry twenty you have racked up since jump school.

You know for sure that the same feeling churns in the guts of everybody, two sticks of eighteen jumpers that line each side of the cavernous C-130.

But what is it that keeps you jumping? It's the fear; in an age when most emotion seems composed of Jell-O, when love is temporary and most lives are empty of valid meaning, this fear and this risk is real. Your life has meaning because you have dared to risk it for something that is worthwhile.

It has become cliché. It is almost embarrassing to say it. "That freedom shall not perish from the earth." Certainly that is why you and thirty-five others will launch yourself into the cold night sky.

Also it's fun.

It's about an hour out now and Lieutenant George Lee, who sits beside you, nudges you to get into your rig. Lee is a little guy and you wonder how he got here, until he smiles. It is the hard smile of a little man who has pushed himself to the utmost, and beyond, to get the senior parachutist wings and the Ranger tab. It's a friendly enough smile, just confident.

"Time to chute up," he says. You reach down and open the heavy canvas kit bag and pull out the chute and the reserve. It takes about ten minutes to get it on and help Lee into his. Then the jumpmaster helps you rig your rucksack under the reserve and checks the drop line, fifteen feet of nylon webbing to lower the rucksack to the ground first, so it doesn't land on top of you.

Your carbine is strapped under the waistband of your chute with the muzzle pointing down. The muzzle and receiver have been covered to prevent dirt, or in this case snow, from getting inside the weapon. The chute and reserve weigh about sixty pounds. The rucksack weighs fifty-five more, the carbine six. That is 121 pounds in all.

Sitting back down, you look down and wonder if there is really a man under all that equipment.

The jumpmaster keeps holding up his fingers, twenty minutes out, ten minutes out. And there is nothing to do now but sit there and let the tension build. It does until you could swear there is no blood in your veins, only adrenaline. Six minutes out.

The crew chief opens the doors and the previously warm aircraft becomes suddenly cool, then chilly, then bitter cold. The jumpmaster stands up in the rear of the aircraft. "Get ready!" he says. Ready? You can't wait to get out the door and end this tension. You have to jump now. It's the only thing that will relax you.

"Stand up!" You have yourself to your feet and look around. All the lights are out except the red "no jump" lights by the door and in the tail of the aircraft. Looking out the door is like looking through a time machine, or into a television set showing something a thousand miles away that has nothing to do with you.

"Hook up!" You take the snap link of your static line from the top of your reserve and hook it into the anchor line cable. It locks itself onto the cable automatically and then for good measure you hook in a safety wire, still thinking about the outside.

Inside you are the darling of the airways, a passenger, surrounded by a million dollars' worth of machine. Inside you sit and go fast. Outside you walk and go slow. Inside the smooth metal walls press around you. Outside there is an infinity of black space with stars like diamonds scattered over black velvet. Inside is claustrophobia; outside is agoraphobia. The only time in your life your status changes faster than this is when you are born.

"Check static lines!" You run your hand down George Lee's static line and the guy behind you checks yours. No snags, no catches.

"Check equipment!" Nope, everything's okay. "Sound off for equipment check!" From the back of the stick comes the count. "Eighteen okay! Seventeen okay!" Working all the way to the front. Each count is accompanied by a slap on the rump of the man in front, just in case he can't hear over the roar of the engines or his own thoughts, whichever are louder.

The jumpmaster moves into the door now and looks outside to pick up the DZ markings, number-ten cans filled with burning gasoline arranged in the shape of an L.

With no lights in the aircraft but the red "no jump" lights the interior has a red aura. When the light changes to green you know it. The jumpmaster goes out, then the next man. The stick starts to shuffle forward like a train leaving the station. Then faster. You get closer. Then the man in front of you disappears. One moment he is standing in the door and the next he is gone.

"Wait a minute. What am I . . . One thousand, two thousand, three thousand, four thousand."

Even while your mind said no your body was going out the door. Faster than it can be said you feel the wind blow your body horizontal and the ties that hold your parachute together snapping to release the canopy.

You check the canopy. Okay. Then you start looking for other jumpers. You have to pull on your left risers to slip away from a parachutist on your right. You hit the quick release on your rucksack and it drops to the end of its fifteen-foot drop line, jerking you slightly in the harness.

The ground is coming up fast and you grab the risers, bend your knees, and get your feet together. No time to enjoy the ride. Don't look down, fool. Keep your eyes on the horizon.

Plop, the rucksack. WHAP, your feet hit the ground, followed all too quickly by the rest of you, rolling automatically into a parachute landing fall.

A few bruises, but that's all, no sprains, no breaks. You release your chute harness and roll out of it. It takes a minute or two to get the chute in the kit bag.

You pause for a moment to catch your breath. Your

knees are still shaking slightly, the long shuddering release from tension. It's funny. The lights on the hills of Seoul look just like San Francisco from here. There is a momentary pang of homesickness, but there is no time.

You look at your watch, grasp the carbine in your hand, and trudge off in the snow. There is still a long night ahead.

# Chinese Fire Drill

For the first time in two months we had no patrols out. U.S. Special Forces detachment A-424 would be in camp for a few days, and we all needed to make a jump or lose jump pay. This was the spring of 1964, a year before the first American troop units came. The first antiwar demonstrations were still two years away. There were maybe twelve thousand Americans in Vietnam.

After 1965 airborne troops in Vietnam drew jump pay on certificates of nonavailability of aircraft. But in '64 we had to make the jumps.

Captain Crews McCulloch, our CO, sent a message to Pleiku, asking for a chopper and fourteen chutes.

"Why fourteen?" I asked, pulling up a chair across from where he sat in our thatch-roofed mess hall, figuring our accounts and drinking coffee.

He looked up from the Ops fund ledger, a square-faced, broad-shouldered Missouri farmer. Captain Mac was as straight and decent a man as I have ever met, but he had a Machiavellian turn of mind. "Twelve of us on the team; Khue and Cowboy want to jump. That makes fourteen," he responded.

Captain Le Van Khue was our camp commander. Technically our team was assigned as advisors to his. But his

Vietnamese team did nothing, and our Montagnard troopers, mountain tribesmen hated by the Vietnamese, took orders directly from the Americans.

Khue himself was a Montagnard in the Vietnamese Special Forces, which was an unenviable thing to be. The Vietnamese army had forgotten him. He hadn't been paid for six months and had to operate a little company store in camp to make enough to feed his family. He usually went barefoot, and wore old camouflage fatigues, worn until they had bleached almost white. He was always dirty, usually drunk, and badly needed to trim his nasal hair.

The other Montagnards said that in his youth he had been a hell of a man, but age, liquor, and neglect had ruined him. Still, once in a while he surprised us, as when he announced he wanted to jump. It all had to do with Cowboy's enthusiasm.

Cowboy was our newest interpreter. He had come into camp with a letter from the past commander of the American Special Forces team at Chu Dron. He was a terrific interpreter, spoke several Montagnard dialects, French, English, Thai, and Lao, plus a little Chinese. But he had antagonized the Vietnamese by eagerly going on combat patrols, and had been fired. The Vietnamese Special Forces in that camp were cowards and he made them look bad. Ours didn't care how they looked.

Cowboy hated Vietnamese and refused even to admit he could speak their language.

If Cowboy was going to jump, Khue had no choice but to go along or lose face.

"Bill and I were kind of hoping you'd let us jump our own," I said.

The Old Man took another sip of coffee. "You know it's against regulations to skydive in Vietnam," he said.

"Well, sir, this wouldn't be exactly skydiving; it would be, sort of, you know . . . free-falling."

"Definitely not." He went on back to drinking his coffee,

and I tore open the plastic bag of one of a stack of New York Sunday *Times* my folks had sent. At least I'd get in one book review before I returned to my requisitions.

The door opened and Kpa Doh, our senior interpreter, entered, coming to a sloppy, but earnest, attention in front of the Old Man. "Please, sir," he said, "I must see you."

Kpa Doh was handsome, dark skinned, a Frank Sinatra fan who had met his wife when they sang propaganda duets in praise of the Diem regime, which they both hated, on the government radio in Banmethuot.

His wife was the most beautiful Montagnard woman I have ever seen, and an accomplished nurse. Bill delivered her first baby while Kpa Doh was on patrol with Captain Mac. She became hysterical, wanted us to stop the patrol and bring him back. She was in no danger, but she wanted her husband. Obviously I couldn't abort the mission, but I did arrange for her to talk to Kpa Doh over the radio.

"Sure," Captain Mac said. "What is it?" He regarded Kpa Doh seriously, but with a humorous quirk to his mouth.

"You make jump tomorrow?"

The Old Man admitted that we would.

"If Cowboy jumps, then I must jump. I am chief interpreter."

That sobered Captain Mac. Kpa Doh was right; he would lose face if Cowboy jumped and he didn't.

"Well, we have fourteen jumpers, and fourteen chutes ordered. We already promised Cowboy. He has jumped before and you haven't."

"If he jumps, then I must jump," Kpa Doh said.

"Yes, well, we'll see."

A Ford Bronco pulled up outside. Captain Dick Waite and John Albertson got out. Captain Mac sighed. Albertson was the provincial USAID representative, and a bit of a grouch. He had won my heart, though, when he pulled strings to get us a chopper to evacuate a critically wounded Montagnard woman.

Captain Waite's young-old face was split by a smile. He was the only member of the local provincial advisory team that we held in high regard. As he came through the squeaking screen door he snapped off his army baseball cap. "I hear you're going to jump tomorrow," he said in his soft, precise voice.

"News sure travels fast," McCulloch said. He could see what was coming.

"You reckon we could tag along?"

"Not me," said Albertson. "I'm getting too old for that stuff."

Captain Mac took another sip of his coffee and asked, "Major Judah say you can jump?"

"Nope. If I asked him, he'd say no, so why ask?"

"Won't you get in trouble?"

Waite shook his head. His grin became broader. "Not very likely. Next week I report in as a battalion advisor to the 9th Division. There won't be any jumping down there in the Delta." He had sought this change of assignment for some time, a chance to advise a real combat outfit.

I grinned, got up, and shook his hand. "Dick," I said, "that's great. Congratulations!"

Captain Mac shook his hand too.

"Sir," I said, "this seems like the least we can do."

Captain Mac folded his arms and cocked his head to one side, thinking. "How many rigs you and Foody have, anyway?"

"Well, let's see. I have a Double L and a single T. Bill's got a C-9 canopy packed in a T-10 backpack, a T-10 canopy in a B-12 backpack with a TU cut in it, a complete T-10 with a badly torn canopy. But the tears are all covered with green tape. He's got two TUs and—"

"Never mind all that. You can jump your own rigs, then?"

"Oh, sure," I said. "Yes, sir. There's no sweat on that."

He turned back to Waite. "How long since you've jumped?"

"Eight years."

"And Kpa Doh, you've never jumped before, right?"

"That is correct, sir."

He turned to me. "You reckon you can give Kpa Doh two weeks of jump school this afternoon, and Captain Waite a refresher course at the same time?"

"Yes, sir. We'll use the grease rack in the motor pool for a PLF platform, and simulate door exits off the side of it. I just need five minutes to get ready and we'll be in business."

I tore out the door and double-timed over to the dispensary. Bill was inside, bandaging a hand wound. "We're in," I said. "The Old Man says we can free-fall."

Bill was our junior medic, a big good-looking redheaded guy, Sp-4 Bill Foody. He had been an engineering student for three years, then decided he did not want to be an engineer, dropped out, and joined the army to mark time.

Before the army Bill had been a skydiver, and that, his intelligence, and educational level made him a natural for Special Forces.

He was miles ahead of me as a jumper. I had made a few static-line jumps with a skydiving club before I went to the army jump school, but I had never been able to get the necessary two jumps in one day that would allow me to free-fall on a Stateside drop zone. But I had convinced Bill I was ready, and he was willing to jumpmaster my first one here in Vietnam.

He turned to me for a moment. "That's great," he said. Then, as an afterthought, he asked, "Does he know you've never jumped free-fall before?"

I grinned. "He never asked, and I didn't bring it up."

• • •

The next morning our team sergeant, Ed Thomas, stood with hands on his hips, a GI bush hat jammed down over his nose. He regarded the small formation by our chopper pad with a jaundiced eye. "My Gawd," he said, "I don't know which this looks more like, an airborne operation or a Chinese fire drill."

The Old Man lined up his first stick of jumpers in front of the UH1B that had brought our chutes from Pleiku, heavy canvas aviator's kit bags laid out in front of them, open and waiting for the parachutists to take out their rigs. Khue was not only dried out, he was bleached. Fear was the first sober expression I ever saw on his face. Kpa Doh looked grim too.

Khue reached down and pulled his chute out, confidently. But he had only jumped French parachutes before, and this rig was completely different. His face went all baffled as he fumbled with the unfamiliar equipment.

Ken Miller, our senior commo man, a ruggedly handsome man in his mid-forties, and I, sat in the jeep, with signal panels and smoke grenades in back, waiting to go out and set up the Drop Zone.

We wouldn't have missed seeing Khue and Kpa Doh chute up for anything. Captain Mac and Slattery, our wiseass demolition sergeant, were going to put them out, and follow them out the door.

Khue swung the T-10 over his back, but he didn't know how to put it on. He stood with his risers twisted, leg straps dangling, a pained, helpless expression on his debauched brown face. Kpa Doh's chute still lay in his kit bag.

"Hey, Sergeant Thomas," I said. "We better get going." He shook his head and piled into the jeep. Ken put it in gear and headed for the camp gate.

The drop zone was a big rice field on the river side of a dirt highway, about two miles from camp, and two miles the other way from Cheo Reo, the provincial capital. The heat was fierce.

Ken parked in the shade of a fair-sized rice hootch. I got out and reached back for the panels. Ken licked his finger and held it up. " 'Bout a three-knot wind," he said. "We can set up anywhere."

We walked a hundred meters into the stubbled rice field and started laying out a big T with the cerise side of the panels up. Then Ken took one of the flank panels to one side of the field and Thomas took the other one to the other side. I went back to the jeep for some smoke grenades.

The Montagnards had seen teams before ours jump, and as soon as we got the panels out they started appearing out of the nearby thatch-roofed villages, nimbly descending the notched logs that served as stairs for their stilted long-houses. The men stood, mostly with loincloths drawn up between their buttocks, legs dusty to the knees. But times were changing, and some wore western clothes. They were impassive, quiet.

This close to town the women wore shiny black sarongs, and blouses. A few miles farther out they went bare-breasted. Protestant missionaries had brought blouses to the Central Highlands.

The kids, too, were still, clutching their mothers' legs or cradled in their fathers' arms, waiting for the show.

My prejump adrenaline flashed like an amphetamine rush.

There was a rising *whop-whop-whop* and the huey appeared over the camp, gaining altitude. By then there must have been two hundred people standing around in the rice field with us. I wanted to tell them to get off our DZ; it's difficult enough to pick out a good spot to land without people running around under you.

A big cloud of dust came roaring out from town. It was Albertson's Bronco wagon pulling into our field to park by our truck. Getting out of the cab he gave the air an aloof sniff. Waite got out on the passenger side and loped around the vehicle.

"When's the first lift coming out?" Albertson asked.

He lit a cigarette disdainfully, to show he wasn't impressed, had seen it all before.

"Probably make one pass over the T, just to check the DZ, then come around for the jump."

"Unnh!"

"Where's the chutes?" Waite asked.

"Rest of the team will be out in the three-quarter in a couple of minutes. They're bringing them."

The crowd on the DZ had grown to at least three hundred, and clusters of people congregated wherever they could find a little shade. The Reed family, Christian and Missionary Alliance missionaries, parked their Land-Rover by the fence on the highway, and stood under a big tree, four hundred feet down the line of flight. Their kids were home for spring vacation. I could barely make out the littlest boy, perched on Bob's shoulders. The oldest boy and girl stood beside Bob. There were four blond heads, Bob and the kids', and Bobbie's brunette.

Even though they had convinced the Montagnard women to wear blouses, I was glad to see them. They, our team, and Albertson were collaborating on a project to build a village for lepers in the province. Our tribe of Montagnards, the Jarai, had the world's highest incidence of leprosy; six of every thousand people had it. I had come to like and respect the Reeds very much.

By the time the chopper made its first pass over the DZ, our operation had become an air show. Then the three-quarter-ton truck drove up and the rest of the team bounced out, throwing parachute-laden kit bags off the back. Foody grabbed three and dragged them over toward me.

Behind the team three-quarter came another one, badly battered and off alignment. Cowboy had brought it with him from Chu Dron. He wore shades, GI bush hat low on his nose, a cowboy roll to the brim. Between his teeth he lightly held a smoking Salem, a mannerism I think he had picked up from James Dean in *Rebel Without a Cause*. His wife and two-year-old daughter, Marina, sat proudly beside him in the front seat. Cowboy's wife had a dark, sullen beauty, and streaks of red in her hair.

The chopper completed its rise and made one pass over the DZ, then circled and lined up for the jump. Bill and I set down the chutes, and I threw out a yellow smoke grenade to indicate that it was okay to drop. Then, as they passed over the T, the first man came out. There was a long pause, and the second came, followed by the last two. The umbilical of their static lines broke their backpacks open and dragged the chutes out in a long arc as they fell out of the rotor wash of the helicopter, then flipped their canopies loose and they started to breathe and inflate. The canopies popped into domes; their descent seemed to stop for a second, and then start again, slowly.

One, two, three, four, they strung out across the sky, great, green, downfloating blossoms. The winds aloft must have been greater than they were on the ground, because the first two started moving out fast, and the last two took up a big one-riser slip back toward the target. The first man went all the way off the drop zone and into the trees on the other side. The second headed toward the big tree where the Reeds were standing. It must have been one of the 'Yards, because he just hung in the harness, making no attempt to slip or get ready to land.

"Get your feet and knees together," I bellowed. "Get your feet and knees together; get your feet and knees together. Get your feet and . . . Forget it!" He came in loose and hit like a sack of mud. But in a moment he was up and running around the chute.

The Old Man and Slattery came in only about a hundred feet from the T and started rolling up their rigs. Bill and I got into ours.

"Okay, go over the procedure one more time," he said to me as he threw his pack on his back.

"Right!" I replied. "I exit, take up a good free-fall body position, back arched hard, arms and legs out to the sides, head way back. Then I count to five thousand and pull. Simple." I tightened my leg straps and tied my reserve parachute down.

"Yeah," he said. "Don't get hypnotized by the pull. You concentrate on that body position. I guarantee you won't forget to pull, but if your position's bad and you go into a spin, you could twist your canopy all the way to the top, and then you might as well not have one."

"Right! Right! Body position."

Captain Mac came walking in, kit bag with parachute inside slung over one shoulder.

"Who was the first man out?" I asked.

"Khue."

"He went in the woods, over there across the road."

"I saw him. Anybody go after him?"

"Yes, sir. About eight or nine 'Yards went over that way. Kpa Doh's all right. He came in by that tree down there. Ought to be here in just a minute."

One more stick went out, and then it was our turn. Waite was chuted up and I helped Cowboy into his rig. They both wore standard T-10 parachutes, and U.S. Army steel helmets. Foody and I had our free-fall rigs and motorcycle helmets. He had on a pair of jeep goggles and I had welder's goggles over my glasses. The chopper came back around and settled to the ground, bouncing on its skids, sending great showers of dust and dry rice stubble into the air. We half ran, half waddled over to the chopper, and put Cowboy and Waite in first.

I secured their static lines to the cargo tie-down rings in the floor of the aircraft while Foody arranged for a second pass at 4,500 feet for him and me.

Waite was first man in the door, then Cowboy, I had briefed Waite on how to sight on the target with his feet, keeping his heels together and the toes turned out, holding the legs straight down against the wind. When the target appeared between his toes it was time to go. Then, over his shoulder, I saw the ground drop away beneath. The clusters of 'Yards below followed our ascent with open-mouthed fascination. Then we were too high and all I could see were the trees off to the front, and the Song Ba river winding down between them.

The wind swirled around in the aircraft, but with goggles I could see without my eyes watering. The pilot had the pattern now, and his trip around was short and precise. I stood up and leaned over Waite's shoulder. We flew in a straight line down Highway 14, a little over to the right to line up with the T. It seemed funny to see people wandering around like little bugs on the ground.

When we got close Waite gave a little hitch of his butt, and I knew he was ready. Then he was gone. He had been blocking the wind, and the blast caught me a stinging blow in the face.

I motioned Cowboy into the door. He moved up, then seemed to hesitate for a second. "GO!" I bellowed.

Foody applied a 10½D to the small of his back, and he disappeared.

The pilot swung off to the left and started climbing. I had no instruments, so I leaned over and looked at Bill's. He showed 1,500 feet on the altimeter mounted to the top of his reserve, but my adrenaline was up and I wanted to get into the door. I forced myself to be calm.

In spite of Bill's comments about body position, I couldn't help wondering if I would be one of those guys who froze once they got out there, just ride it all the way in without pulling.

I looked over at Bill's altimeter again: 3,500. *Goddammit, how long is this going to take?* I breathed in great gulps. It became cold inside the aircraft as we climbed, and the wind whipped my face. I started to move into the door.

Bill grabbed my shoulder and tapped his altimeter. It read 4,000.

"Remember," he shouted. "Body position."

"Yeah, yeah, yeah!" I said irritably. Then he moved me toward the door.

I scooted into the door and hung my feet into the blast, looking at the ground below. The drop zone was much smaller now, and I could barely make out people on it. I thought of the skydiver's maxim, "The time to pull is when the people look like ants. When the ants look like people, it's too late." Bill slapped my shoulder. I pushed off.

I was out, in the uncontrolled fall before you reach terminal velocity and stabilize, counting. "One thousandtwothousandthreesnfrthsnfisn—land and sky blurred together. Hand clawed for the rip cord, I slapped my left shoulder four times without getting a grip on it, and then I was falling head down, looking in amazement at the thing in my hand.

There was a tug at my back, followed immediately by a jerk that ripped at my inner thighs and almost somersaulted me backwards through my risers. I hung there, shaking, wondering where to put the rip cord. I finally wrapped the cable and pins around the handle and put it in my fatigue pants pocket, then reached for my toggles and tried to locate the target. I was already over it, so I turned and faced into the wind as the ground grew larger and larger until it was almost life size. I focused my eyes on the horizon so I wouldn't tense up at the last minute, and got my feet and knees together.

My feet hit and my legs crumpled; I flopped over, caught myself on my thigh, and my back and helmet slammed into the ground. For me a normal landing. I got up just in time to watch Foody come in. He was doing beautifully, coming straight for the target. Fifty feet in the air, and forty feet back from the target he turned and faced the wind to prevent an overshoot.

The wind failed him and he dropped straight down through a thorn tree. He wasn't hurt, but the beautiful orange and white canopy, which he owned himself, and had paid good money for, was pierced by about five thousand thorns.

I rolled up my rig and walked over. He stood, hand on one hip, head cocked, looking at the mess in the tree.

"How was my body position?" I asked.

"Pretty good. You started to spin, but caught yourself and straightened out," he said. "Jesus, look at that!" He went over and unsnapped his capewells, to get the backpack loose. Then he climbed up the tree and started to pick the chute off, thorn by pointy thorn. I went over, grabbed the risers, and pulled them back away from the tree as he freed the canopy. I had to be very careful to avoid a rip. A number of nearby 'Yards had gathered to lend an inexpert hand.

"Would you tell them for Christ's sake to keep away," Bill said beseechingly. "They'll ruin it."

Albertson strolled over from his Bronco, with his interpreter, a small, dour Montagnard named Nay Luette. They got some of the 'Yards back from the chute, and we all started working to get it off, while the last lift jumped, the rest of the team took the DZ down, and everybody else loaded up, then went back to camp for a beer.

# Meet Me in the
# Middle of the Air

*Meet me, Jesus, meet me*
*Meet me in the middle of the air*
*And if these wings should fail me, Lord*
*Meet me with another pair.*
*Well, well, well, so I can die easy*
*Well, well, well, so I can die easy*
*Well, well, well, so I can die easy*
*Jesus gonna make up my dyin' bed.*

—JOSH WHITE

We were running across the hard surface of the old Japanese runway while the airplane revved up on the other side. The heavy nylon straps of the parachute harness dug into my crotch and the weight of the backpack and reserve turned the run into a half waddle.

The other jumpers in the stick were running, too, and we formed a loose echelon formation across the wide scarred concrete, all of us waddling awkwardly like the chase scene in a Donald Duck cartoon. Orange coveralls ballooned out over our jump boots as we carried our white leather helmets by the chin straps like buckets.

The aircraft was an Otter, a high-wing single-engine olive-drab job with the stubby utilitarian appearance of a farm tractor. The big radial engine revved and the airplane bucked and slewed on the runway. We ran around to the door and stood there in a mob, the slipstream whipping orange nylon against our legs while Brown, the jumpmaster, pulled us aboard, one by one. I was third and sat in one of the seats across from the door and strapped in.

Inside there were spaces for eight men and we crammed in solid on the heavy canvas bench seats, leaning back against the net that kept us off the bare bulkhead. It was dark except right at the empty doorway and the small circular portholes that filtered light through the net and around the heads of the men on the benches, illuminating an ear and a patch of hair and leaving the rest of the man's face in darkness.

The engine revved louder and then, with a jolt that threw us rearward, we were moving. Through the door the landscape turned into two blurs, a gray concrete one on the bottom and a green grass one on top.

Then the gray one dropped out of sight and the green one slowed down and developed perspective and we could see all the way across the potato patches and the old Japanese taxi strips to the small village of Yomitan, all steep red-tile roofs close together, with green hedges in between, and beyond that Highway One with its insane traffic of three-wheel Mazda trucks, little Nissan taxis, U.S. Army buses, and GI wives in Buicks and bubble hairdos, all moving at the island's snaillike thirty-mile-an-hour speed limit.

Past that climbed the coral mountainous center spine of the island and farther the rice paddies and more villages and then the Pacific Ocean with nothing beyond until Midway.

The airplane banked and turned left. I put welder's goggles over my glasses and strapped the white-leather helmet, with its built-in metal skullcap, over that. The coastline passed underneath. Highway One had bent to run along the coastline and it formed a ribbon between the high cliffs on the right and the slender width of coral beach and the East China Sea. Strange outcroppings of jagged coral lined the

beach and in the mountains the spiny plants grew among
small gnarled trees and hard sharp grass.

We passed over the coast, the shallow inland waters with
greenish patches of coral reef beneath, and then there was
nothing but blue. It didn't look like water. It looked like
pale-blue plastic, rippling softly, with ever-changing hard
yellow glimmers, out on to the horizon, where it faded into
an indiscriminate blur and came back on top a paler blue
with clouds.

The airplane banked and turned left again, and I thought,
*I am calm and calm and calm again,* and breath came in
great gulps through the mouth.

My hand was on the stopwatch over the reserve, winding.
The old nervous, anxious ready-to-go adrenaline feeling
was creeping through my body again, and I could feel that
wolfish grin you wear at the start of a combat patrol coming
back.

The altimeter read thirty-five-hundred feet and it was
cold in the aircraft. I took my right hand off the stopwatch
and put it carefully on the seat. With my left I touched the
rip-cord handle that hung free beside the reserve, then
reached down to check the position of the small orange
knob, called a lollipop, that activates the automatic opening
device.

The airplane banked once more and soon we were flying
over Okinawa again, coastline, military installations, high-
ways, little villages, and the great quarries that bordered the
drop zone. It was about fifty degrees and wind whipped
around in the cabin.

Brown motioned the first man into the door. The other
two got up and I took the number-four position. The other
four jumpers sat waiting for the second pass over the drop
zone. We crouched in line, in a kind of Jackie Gleason
away-we-go posture, left hand on the lollipop, right hand
over the stopwatch. The door was blocked by the number-
one man and it became very dark in the aircraft. Brown

knelt and looked out the door, waiting for the aircraft to pass the exit point. The wind turned his face even redder than usual and fluttered his right cheek. He looked and kept looking and it seemed the moment would never come. I thought, *Goddammit, if we're going to go, let's do it.*

Brown pulled his head back in and motioned the first man. He had not chosen his position well. The first man pulled his lollipop and hurled it into the cabin with one swift motion, smashing Brown right in the mouth. Then he was gone.

The next two caught Brown, too, and his mouth was covered with blood; then I was alone by the door. I whipped mine straight out to the side to miss him and then I was free.

Falling and falling and falling away, head back, arched hard, arms straight out and legs apart, a brief glimpse of paddy and counting, one thousand—Christ, I did it, thousand, three—here it comes, reach for the rip-cord handle thousand and *pull* thousand. Flare again into the cross position for a second before the giant grabs your back and it is all over.

I was hanging in the harness with the T-shaped blast handle in my hand, snaky coil of rip cord dangling, bouncing, from that and the chute moving away from the target.

I reached up, grabbed the risers, and looked up to check the canopy. It was an inverted half globe of nylon, the sun shining through turning the olive drab into a pale evanescent green. The big football shaped opening in back let a constant jet of air escape, driving the chute forward.

Lots of work to do and not much time to do it in. I unhooked the chest strap on the harness and snapped the rip-cord handle into that, freeing both hands. Then reached right hand to left shoulder and vice versa to pull the cords on the two forks that held the risers fixed in their slip rings. The risers free, I grabbed the right rear one and pulled hard. The chute made a U-turn in the air and soon came around in line with the target. I pushed the riser back into its normal position and the chute stopped turning.

It wasn't a very hot rig and I was only getting about six knots forward speed. I was going to come in around a hundred feet short of the big white X of the target on the ground. The potato patch moved by underneath. At a hundred and fifty feet I grabbed the riser again and turned to face into the wind, which slowed the chute enough so that it was dropping almost straight down, with only some backward movement.

The fields became a field and that field developed rows and furrows and weeds, and I brought my feet and knees together, toes pointed down, and reached for the risers. My toes touched, and then right thigh, buttock, back, and I was up and running around to collapse the air out of the chute and to keep it from running with the wind like a giant sail.

When the canopy collapsed it became an olive-drab blob on the ground with twigs and grass tangled in the spaghetti running from it to me. I started unhooking snaps and rolling it up to throw in the heavy canvas bag.

My legs were a little shaky as I threw the kit bag on my back and started hoofing it back to the runway.

The kit bag was heavy and the plowed ground soft and spongy underneath. The aircraft was on the ground again almost half a mile away and the sound was small and thin as it took off with the second stick of jumpers. It circled higher and higher. I stopped and watched, hands over eyes, as it made its final pass across the face of the sun and the exit point. The engine drone deepened as it throttled back, seeming to stand almost still in the air. They should be coming out any second now and the black hole of the empty door was clearly visible.

Where were they? Why don't they—there . . . a small dot appeared beneath the aircraft, then another and then there were four falling, spread out diagonally across the sky. The first fast-falling dot popped and became a slow-falling green blossom as the jumper pulled. The other three blossomed when they came even with him. Then they broke, made their turns, and started their runs toward the target.

I was almost back to the runway when the airplane completed its circle and came back over the exit point to put out the last four jumpers.

They appeared again, four dots beneath the aircraft, and fell for five seconds. The blossoms started appearing, one, two, three, in the order of their exit. I waited for the fourth to appear, but the dot kept falling. It grew larger and developed arms and legs as it neared the ground.

There was no point in yelling. He couldn't hear. But my mouth formed the words, "Pull, babe! Pull! Pull! Pull! Pull!" He went a full twelve seconds and must have been about fifteen hundred feet when his chute was fully deployed.

The airplane was on the ground and idling. Another line of orange-clad jumpers with olive-drab humps on their backs scuttled across the runway. Other jumpers were straggling into the turn-in point, faces flushed, hair soggy with sweat, and dirt from their falls ground into their coveralls.

I handed Montano, the smiling rigger, my rip cord and threw the kit bag in back of the trailer behind the three-quarter-ton truck. "Who was it that opened late?"

"Your buddy, I think," Montano said.

My buddy was an officer I had known since we were both second lieutenants pushing basic trainees through Fort Dix.

I went over to the stack of bagged parachutes and snatched one up for the second jump. Brown was standing by the chutes, nursing his bleeding upper lip with a handkerchief. He was a short, sturdy-looking man in orange coveralls and an Air Force flight jacket, red faced and full of taut, nervous energy that always seemed ready to explode. Normally his mouth carried the signs of a wry, hard humor, but right then he didn't look very humorous with the handkerchief under his nose.

I bent over and unzipped the kit bag and pulled out my fresh chute. "How's the mouth?" I asked, unsnapping the leg straps and laying the rig out to put on.

"Annnhhh!" he said.

"Occupational hazard."

"Grrrmmpf." He walked off toward the rigger truck. I swung the backpack over on my back and folded the kit bag into thirds and snapped it under the leg straps. Then I hooked the chest strap and started looking for somebody to tighten the belly-band on the reserve. One of the guys just coming in cinched it up for me and I started looking through the zipper pockets on the coveralls for cigarettes. There was one entire stick to go before my bunch went up again.

My buddy, the other captain, came over with a kit bag dangling from one hand and his reserve and helmet from the other.

"Was that you took the long delay?"

He nodded. He was a good-looking guy in kind of an ugly way. He had the tight muscular body of a college athlete, which he had been, and a curly blond crew-cut, a wide mouth over strong teeth, and a nose broken in two or three or four places. He was a good man and I would hate to see him have trouble in this course. I didn't ask him what happened. He would tell me if he wanted me to know.

"Thought I had a good position," he said, "but I was all over the sky like a spider. I was on my back and trying to go for the blast handle when the timer got me."

"It's good you were pulling, though. You going up again?"

"Sure."

I was glad. He needed a good jump now that his first one had been bad.

He reached down and unzipped his kit bag and started pulling out the chute. "Wind's coming up," he said.

"It always starts to pick up on this old drop zone around nine-thirty in the morning. Be doing good if we get in one more today."

Montano had the clipboard with him and he called out my stick number from back by the rigger truck. I heaved myself to my feet and started over toward the airplane again.

You're always tired on the second jump and the adrenal glands have done their trick for the day. So you just sit there and when the jumpmaster says get ready, you get ready, and when he says go, you go.

My friend was in the air by the time my chute was turned in. I waited for him and we walked down to the old hardstand where the cars were parked. His was a Rambler wagon and we threw our reserves and helmets in the back and got in the car.

"How'd your second one go?"

He started the car and gunned off the ramp down toward the highway. "Not much better than the first," he said. "I pulled in time, but the position was still bad.

"How the hell am I going to bring my team in from forty thousand feet at night with equipment when I can't even hold a good position on a lousy five-second delay?"

"Don't worry about it. You're probably doing one little something wrong and as soon as you find it you'll straighten right out."

He had that anxious, trying-too-hard look. "I sure hope so," he said. "What's bugging me is I had a buddy go all the way at Bragg last year. Wife and two kids."

"What happened?"

"I don't know. He was skydiving and didn't have a timer. Maybe he got interested in the scenery and just laid out there and watched the trees go by. Anyway, he's dead."

After lunch we went back to the Quonset hut that housed the 1st Special Forces Group (Airborne) High-Altitude-

Low-Opening parachute detachment. HALO they call it.

At one o'clock we were gathered in the classroom. Brown read off the names of the guys who had lost their rip cords that morning and announced that by ancient and honorable custom among free-fall parachutists it was going to cost each a case of beer.

Then we packed. Outside I went to work on the shakeout detail with a staff sergeant and a PFC. We ran the canopies up a long vertical clothesline affair and shook all the grass, dirt, and twigs out of the canopies and suspension lines, then ran them back down again and put them in kit bags to be taken inside and packed.

When the chutes were all shaken out we went inside to help on the tables. There were two teams of students, each working a table, taking out twists, tangles, and turns and flaking out the panels in the canopy into neat leaves of nylon with a clear air channel down the middle for the air to flow in and inflate the chute.

Montano supervised and made the final assembly on one table and Freeman, the frowning rigger, worked on the other. Brown sat on a table at one end of the rigger shed with a stopwatch, awarding points to the first table through. At six-thirty the last chute was packed and we went home with instructions to be back to draw equipment for a drop at five-thirty the next morning.

The next day it was cold and overcast and the airplane was late. There was a little breeze even before the first stick got in the air; nothing really too bad. But it was a steady five knots with gusts to ten and it wasn't going to get any better.

By the time my chute was turned in after the first jump and I was saddled up for the second, the wind was steady at eight, with an occasional gust to fifteen.

Ed Rybat, the officer-in-charge of the HALO committee, said, "Put 'em in the air. If this holds we can jump them. If it gets any worse we'll have to quit."

Bill Cranford was jumpmaster. He crouched in the door with his helmet on, but no goggles, looking like Bob Hope with five o'clock shadow.

There are jumpers who say they are not afraid, but I think they lie. Usually it follows a curve. When you first get on the airplane, you sit there secure in the knowledge that it is all an illusion. Nobody is really dumb enough to do this. Then you go through the bad part, realizing you are going to do it, but not wanting to. Then the adrenaline gets up and you can hardly wait to get out the door. But that day it was off and I had just got to the stage where you don't want to when Cranford motioned us into the door. He held up ten fingers, a ten-second delay, our first. The longest before had been five.

But I didn't want to.

*Ka-blast!* and I was out there hanging on to a whole lot of nothing, right over the rock quarry, counting slowly, one thousand, two thousand. The quarry started over a slow twist to the right. I corrected by bending left, but that was wrong, because I was turning, not the quarry.

Everything melted into a blur and I crabbed. That flipped me upside down and I caught a glimpse of my toes in a vast moving field of blue.

*Pull! Pull! Pull! Pull! Pull!*

Then I was hanging right-side up in the harness and the rip cord was falling away beneath, whirling around in a lazy circle. I clutched with my left hand, but by then it was past my feet and dropping away out of sight toward the khaki-colored quarry below. There went a case of beer.

It took a hard pull to get the forks out of the risers. The canopy bellied in as I grabbed the right rear riser and the chute slowly spun around to face the target.

Beside the X, white smoke from the smoke pot streamed out flat along the ground. Then the ground started moving by underneath very fast.

I had about twenty knots forward speed and was going to overshoot. At eight hundred feet I turned to face into the wind and cut my forward speed, then looked over my shoulder to see where the chute was going to come in.

It was still going to overshoot the target, and if it followed the glide path it had taken, was going right into the runway. I have seen jumpers break both legs on that runway. I turned again, trying to run over.

At two hundred feet I was over the rear end of the runway. Our instructions were that the beginning HALO jumper should turn into the wind at two hundred feet regardless. I turned, held, and got my feet and knees together, expecting to drop backward onto the runway at about eight knots. My knees were shaking and I stared fixedly at the horizon so as not to know the exact moment of impact and tense up.

All that wide concrete runway was coming into the bottom of my field of vision when the balls of my feet crashed into the dirt about two feet on the far side of the runway, and butt and head followed a split second later. It knocked all the wind out and I lay there trying to get some breath while the chute filled up with air. I leaned on one elbow to get up and the chute flipped me over on my belly and dragged me face first through three mouthfuls of nightsoil-fertilized Okinawan potato patch before I could pop the canopy release on the left shoulder. I lay there blowing grimy blood out of my nose and spitting out dirt.

From across the runway I could hear Rybat's voice calling, "Get up, don't lay there. It's too early for siesta."

*Up yours, too, buddy*, I thought as I crawled up, first on feet and knees, and then stood, dusting the crud off my hands and blowing the drying blood out of my nose. Then I started to unsnap and put the chute away.

It was in the bag and on my back by the time the next stick came in. Tony Avgoulis, the HALO supply man, smashed into the ground face first, running with the wind at about twenty knots, and tore his coveralls half off. It broke the crystals out of both his stopwatch and altimeter.

It was just a bad day. They didn't jump anymore.

I ran across my buddy at the turn-in point and asked, "How'd it go?" He was all smiles. "Great! It was really great. How was yours?"

If there had been another jump that day it would have been all right, but we canceled because of the wind. If there'd have been one the next day that would have been fine, too, but it rained.

On the morning of the third day I got up afraid to jump, limping from where I'd smashed in and with a big purple bruise running fourteen inches lengthwise up my right leg. I couldn't work up any enthusiasm for free-fall parachuting that day. The winds were too high and we didn't jump. That night I lay in bed and watched myself whistle all the way in three times, and bounce.

It would be so easy to quit. Just turn in the gear and go back to my desk. Make one static line jump every three months to draw the pay. Nobody would say anything. Nobody would care but me.

I had to take it all the way through the logic of the thing. All right, suppose the worst happens, and you go all the way in. You're dead, right?

Then suppose you quit. You've got to live inside a quitter all your life. Death is a zero. Quitting is a minus. The best deal you can get is to go ahead and jump.

Then I went to sleep.

The next morning it was clear and calm and we drew our gear and loaded the kit bags, with their ready-to-jump chutes in the back of the trailer, and drove on out to the drop zone. The decision to jump had been made. My problem was to do it right. If I clutched again there was no

telling how long it would take me to get the thing straightened out.

I got a kit bag and chuted up, then sat on the runway
watching the first two sticks go up to the airplane, exit, and
float slowly to earth again. The nerves were pretty well
under control, but I had to keep forcing the muscles in the
back of my neck to relax.

Then it was our turn and we were up and running across
the runway again.

In the airplane I went over in my mind the procedure to
follow, then when I was done I went over it again. The
adrenal glands could do what they wanted. The heart could
race, the blood could freeze, but the mind had to be free
and clear and in control.

*All right, when he gives the stand-up, get up, get in line,
left hand on the lollipop, hit the stopwatch, swing the right
foot out the door, and drop straight out with your arms
spread wide in the cross. Arch your back hard. The best
way to check your arch is to look at the jumpmaster on the
way out. Then cock your head to the side and check your
instruments. Hold your position until the time is up and
then come in for the pull. Be sure to come in with both
arms or the wind will catch your right arm and flip you
over on your back.*

*Check canopy, pull the slip-riser forks, and head for the
target. Face into the wind at two hundred feet and get your
feet and knees together.*

*All right, when he gives the stand-up . . .*

He gave the stand-up. I was number-one man and I went
into my Jackie Gleason crouch by the door and watched
the jumpmaster as he knelt there looking for the exit point.
Below was all square, varishaded-green rice paddies.

All the apprehension drained out and I was ready, both
feet planted solidly on the deck plates, mind clear and calm.
He jerked his finger out the door and I whipped out the

lollipop, tapped the stopwatch, swung one gleaming Corcoran jump boot into the rushing air.

There was one good clear glimpse of the jumpmaster's helmet and goggles in the door, directly above and moving away. Then it was all green paddies and blue ocean. The weight of my body disappeared and for that long glorious screaming moment I was freer than the eagles can ever be.

# The Long Hard Fall

Don't get me wrong; I love editing this magazine. But editing, writing, and choosing pictures of people fighting wars and jumping out of airplanes are not the same as doing it. Every so often I have to get out and feel the wind in my face.

I can't get away long enough to squeeze in a war, so when I heard about Gene Mike Bland's Progressive Free-Fall course in Asheboro, North Carolina, I didn't even think about sending someone younger or in better shape. I just bought myself a ticket and headed south.

Mike picked me up at the airport. He was easy to spot by his bulk, his beard, and the Vietnam boonie hat on his head. He also had his son, a skinny towheaded boy of ten or so, tagging along. It was Mike's divorced daddy weekend. I was glad to have the kid, whom Mike introduced as Charles, along. My own boys are almost through high school and live far away. But I miss those divorced daddy weekends.

After six months in New York it was great to be back in America. Woods flowed past the car and telephone lines plunged and rose between the poles as Mike and I felt each other out. We talked about the war and the Silver Star he got when he stacked up over a hundred NVA in front of his M60.

We talked about parachuting. Mostly he talked and I listened. This was a man with over five thousand jumps, a veteran of both the Golden Knights, the Army's World Champion parachute team, and the HALO Committee, which teaches free-fall as an infiltration technique. In most company I can kind of swagger around and appear modestly casual about being a master blaster, but compared to Mike I was practically a novice.

Mike and Charles had been at the Astroid DZ all day and hadn't eaten, so he stopped and they each had a foot-long and a chocolate shake (Charles's choice) and I had a cup of coffee.

It was way past dark when we got to Mike's home, an old church he has converted into nine-tenths rigger shed and one-tenth living quarters. The place was about as neat as most bachelor quarters are, which is not very. It reminded me more of an artist's studio than anything else, only instead of paints and canvas frames and completed pictures, this place was full of multicolored canopies, backpacks, packing tables, and skydiving trophies.

In the yard next door was a perfectly normal seven-room tract house with a Plymouth in the drive and a bass boat under the carport. "What do your neighbors think of all this?" I asked.

"They think I'm crazy," he replied without hesitation.

That night Charles slept in Mike's bed. I slept on one of the packing tables and Mike slept out on the ground, rolled up in a poncho. This seemed a perfectly reasonable procedure to all of us.

But this scroungy arrangement was a classic illustration of something I have long held to be true, that all of western civilization, all civilization as a matter of fact, is simply the total effect of all those guys, each showing off for some woman. Left to ourselves all men would do is hunt, fish, and kill each other off for the fun of it.

For a man there are only two reasons to go indoors, to get laid and to make money. There is only one reason to make money.

Oddly enough that's all most of us ever do. We just dream about the rest.

The next morning Mike made flapjacks and bacon. I asked him how he had become a drop-zone operator in the first place. I know of no more precarious way to make a living. Running a DZ had obviously not put him on easy street, and he obviously didn't give a shit.

What he told me simply confirmed my theory. He had been an aeronautical engineer with a four-bedroom house in the suburbs, a terminally shaky marriage, and a shrink to tell him he wasn't happy. The reason he went to the shrink in the first place was to save the marriage. "But one of the questions she asked me was 'What do you really want to do?' " he quoted over a third cup of coffee.

" 'You bitch about everything and nothing suits you. What do you really want to do?' "

"I said, 'I want to jump out of airplanes.' "

"She said, 'Well, why don't you?' and I thought about it, and here I am."

After breakfast Mike, Charles, and I rode in his surplus M155 jeep ambulance out to the DZ. By any standards other than ostentatious living Mike has to be considered a success. Hell, the man owns two airplanes and an airport. It's a small airport with a mobile-home rigger-shack/office, a hanger with a pitched roof, a grass strip, and a windsock, but an airport nonetheless.

Mike's partner, Bev Werner, was sitting on the steps in front of the trailer with her chin in her hand when we arrived. We were supposed to have been there a half hour before, but I had held us up with my questions.

Bev started out as one of Mike's students, and eventually skydiving took over her life.

Mike ran me through a few PLFs and we were ready to go.

Just before we took off it occurred to me that, although I have been skydiving off and on for over twenty years, I had never before jumped with anyone who had over five hundred jumps. Bev had twice as many parachute jumps as anyone I'd ever jumped with before, and Mike had five times as many as she did.

The plan was that Mike, taking advantage of the fact that I was a fairly experienced jumper, was going to put me through an accelerated version of his course. I was to attempt a seven- to eleven-jump course in four jumps over the weekend and be back in the office by Tuesday at the latest.

For myself I wanted to do a story that would take the reader deep into the skydiver's world.

About once every five years some reporter does the story of how he or she goes out to the DZ, makes his or her first static-line jump, and lands in a tree, but, boy, was it thrilling!

I wanted to go deep into the world of the long fall, the square parachute, and the multiman hookup.

Three times I'd been on the edge of that world. I'd quit once to go to Vietnam as a soldier, once to go to Cambodia as a correspondent and free-lance guerrilla-warfare advisor, and once because I'd broken my leg badly enough to keep me in a cast for almost a year.

This course should put me back on the edge in two days.

The course is, in a way, an outgrowth of the Army's HALO (High-Altitude–Low-Opening) program. In a normal skydiving course of instruction the student makes five static-line jumps, a few hop-and-pops, a few five-second delays, a few ten- and twenty-second delays, and rarely goes beyond a thirty-second fall from 7,500 feet.

In HALO, now, they take an already qualified military parachutist, throw him out at 20,000 feet, and let him make and correct all his mistakes at once.

The U.S. Parachute Association, the semiofficial guardian of U.S. jumpers, has okayed an accelerated free-fall course built somewhat on the HALO model, in which a first-time jumper goes out at 10,000 feet with two instructors hanging on to his harness. The student very quickly, say in ten or fifteen jumps, achieves a level of proficiency greater than that which I achieved back in the old days with my sixty-five free-falls.

Mike has somewhat modified the USPA course, in that he starts a first-time jumper off with the five static-line jumps that are normal under the conventional method. That is also the same number, if not the same type, as to qualify as a military parachutist.

On the way up I was calm and happy in the airplane. It hadn't been that way the day before. On the way to the Newark Airport I was as scared as I've ever been in my life. If I jump a lot it becomes routine, but this was my first free-fall in five years, the second after having broken both bones in my ankle, straight across. Since then all I'd made were three military static-line jumps with the Royal Thai Special Forces.

My fear on the way to the airport had not been uncontrolled, but it had been huge.

There were plenty of solid reasons to be scared: 1) I was forty-six years old, 2) I had let my weight get up to 210, 3) although I had been working out and had planned to get my run back up to five miles the week before, I had instead worked three days to get the magazine out when I should have been home in bed with the summer flu.

On the plus side I would be jumping a Para-Commander, which I'd done many times before, and, properly controlled, a PC will set you down like jumping off your porch. I wasn't *that* out of shape.

On the bus to the airport, filled with a fear that would have panicked anyone who didn't know it like an old enemy, I weighed these factors carefully, then made my decision based on a simple desire to jump from 10,000 feet, something I had wanted to do for years.

*Fuck it!* I thought. *I'm goin',* and thought no more about it.

A climb to 7,500 feet used to seem to me like it took forever, but for some reason this climb to 10,500 did not. I fiddled with my helmet and goggles a bit, and traded confident winks and smiles with Mike, Bev, and Larry Riddle, the photographer. The next thing I knew the ground was way way below, not the familiar checkerboard, more like a map without grid lines. Mike opened the door and a big wind sucked all the warmth out of the aircraft. The pilot turned and headed down the wind line.

Mike made a few gestures to the pilot, to line him up exactly like he wanted, and then he climbed out on the step and hung from the wing strut. Bev motioned me into the door and I fought the wind to keep my feet on the step. I knew the wind was running ripples across my cheeks because I had seen it on others so many times before.

Bev motioned me out onto the step and I climbed out there, full into the blast. The horizon curved and the ground was far below and hazy.

Bev climbed out on the step beside me and gave me a nod. The exit was under my control. I rocked back twice to signal I was ready, rocked again, and pushed off. We went off the aircraft in a clump, Bev and Mike clutching my harness.

We were just doing the drill for the first long fall on this jump. They would stay with me all the way down to four grand, tap me back into place if I went unstable, and pull my rip cord if I forgot how. Fat chance of that. There was no problem with having them there, any more than you feel the weight of your tanks in a scuba dive.

There was no weight, just a buoyant feeling and a big wind in my face. My sleeves fluttered.

The first part of the drill was three dummy rip-cord pulls. Mike gave me the nod and I came in for the cord, pulling my left arm over my head to keep from going unstable.

After every DRCP I went through a drill controlled by the code word GASP; check the *ground,* check your *altimeter,* down somewhere around nine-five by this time, check the *secondary* jumpmaster, check the *primary* jumpmaster, get his nod, and go back in for another DRCP.

The *ground* part was awesome. The rest was a quick series of stills, altimeter, Bev's face, Mike's face right in mine.

Just after I completed the last DRCP Larry flashed diagonally from my upper left field of vision, pulled up about twenty feet out, and lay there, snapping with his helmet camera.

The only remaining part of the drill was to stretch out, extend my arms and legs as far as I could and still keep stable. Mike gave me the signal, sort of like an upside-down peace sign, with the fingers wiggled. I stretched out and came back in. It was easy.

When I came back in from the last drill we were at about five-two and the ground below was starting to look familiar, but I still had twelve seconds till cord time. I just lay out there and rode that tall column of air, enjoying the luxury of the extra altitude, gloating that I hadn't lost it.

At about four-five I did the GASP drill again and Mike nodded for me to pull. I went in for the cord, felt a tug at my back and then, WHAP, the inside of my thighs stung and I looked up to see a pretty blue PC canopy.

Bev, Mike, and Larry dropped away another thousand feet before they opened, tiny squares far below. The reason for the student to open at four grand is so that, if for some reason he fails to do so, the jumpmaster will have plenty of time to do it for him. If they get separated, the chute has an automatic timer anyway. There is plenty of safety cushion built into this system.

I reached up and grabbed the right toggle, in this case a soft nylon ring, and oriented myself toward the target. Mike had his toggles set about a foot higher than I was used to, and I just put them where they were comfortable and forgot about it, jockeying toward the target.

I have never been much of an accuracy freak. For me the thrill is in the fall, not in turning myself into a human dart. What I've always done is head for the target and then turn into the wind and hold at two hundred feet, wherever I am.

But in Mike's system he lands on the target and signals you in.

I picked him out and started following his directions. As I got closer I could see him kind of pushing his hands straight up, but I couldn't figure out what he meant by that, so I ignored it, kept the toggles where I was used to them, and kept jockeying. Hot damn, an almost perfect jump. I was even going to be right on the edge of the target. I got my feet and knees together and watched that pretty green grass come up and then locked my eyes on the horizon. . . .

Oh, shit, it hurt. Oh, shit, oh shit, oh shit! Flat on my back and not even sure yet that I broke something, but hurt for sure.

Jumpers came running from across the DZ.

I called Kat from the hospital and told her that my pelvis was broken. I was busted, hurting badly, and bleeding inside. Twenty-three years of jumping, and not only the worst parachuting accident I've ever had, but tied for the worst I've ever seen. One of the Americans had broken his pelvis on that first jump in Thailand last year. He didn't act like he liked it any better than I did.

With that infinite tenderness for which she is so well known, Kat said, "When your ass is well enough, I'm going to kick it up between your shoulder blades."

Kat's premonitions are usually good, and she had begged me not to make this jump. She had a dream the night before I left that my midsection was eaten in two by rats. She figured that meant I was going to buy the farm, but when she saw she couldn't talk me out of it, she kissed me good-bye, did it right, and smiled.

I think a good woman has to have more guts and class than any man. God had made men so that they can be fools and get away with it. Women can't.

It certainly wasn't Mike's fault that I splattered. I got the only broken bone they ever had on his DZ. I just let myself get overweight and out of shape, and then made the canopy unstable by pulling the toggles too low. It oscillated just before I hit, crammed my left leg into the socket it sets in, and snapped it in two places.

I don't know if I'll ever jump again or not. In a sense it's irresponsible for a man with dependents and sloppy habits to fall from the sky. On the other hand, every so often something comes over me and nothing will do but what I strap on a parachute and hurl my ancient airborne ass out of an airplane.

# POW/MIA

# POW/MIA

In the veterans' community there is no issue that strikes deeper than POW/MIA. In Vietnam I feared capture more than death, as did, I think, most of us. The thought of our guys still held prisoner there fifteen to twenty-five years later makes me crazy. And yet there is nothing we can do, and very little our government can do. We monitor the situation, we wait; we look for an opening. We will never, we cannot, quit, abandon hope, or abandon the issue.

Rumors are rampant. It is rumored that the Americans remaining in Vietnam fall into three groups: 1) GI criminals who were on the lam and couldn't get out. These people are alleged to be living among the populace, to have jobs and families. 2) Actual POWs who have understandably given up hope of coming home, accepted paroles, and who also live among the populace, and have jobs and families, and 3) hard cases who are still imprisoned.

It is further rumored that the French are still buying back individual prisoners from the Indochina War, and that they hide them in their former colonies to avoid blowing the deal. There is a rumor that the U.S. government is doing the same thing, and putting returned POWs into something like the Witness Protection Program, so the Vietnamese will not be embarrassed and close off this supposed conduit.

Another rumor is that the previous rumor was floated by the government to keep the veterans quiet.

In the final analysis nobody knows anything for absolutely certain except that a number of POWs who were known to be held were never returned, and have never been accounted for.

But a number of interesting facts have come to light through the investigations of various interested groups. It has been learned, for instance, that the Soviets, our supposed allies in WWII, never returned the American prisoners they captured when they took over the stalags in East Germany. After the Katyn massacre we wouldn't return any more unwilling Eastern European soldiers and in retaliation Stalin kept several hundred American GIs, some of whom may still be prisoners in the Gulag. Nor did the Chinese return a fairly large number of American prisoners from Korea.

Why keep them?

Presuming that there are still living POWs, the Vietnamese originally held them as bargaining chips for recognition and reparations. At the Paris Peace Accords they promised not to take over South Vietnam right away, and we promised reparations. Neither promise was kept.

# Vigil for a Missing Son

Very low, two Navy A-6 Intruders flicked over the triple-canopy jungle. Mile after mile of variegated green trees rolled under the planes' bellies. They flew too fast, in the fading light, to recognize individual terrain features, to know if it was a river or a hidden fifteen-foot waterfall that flashed by below.

In the right-hand seat of the left-hand aircraft, with his eyes on the scope, Nick Brooks couldn't see outside. He was functioning as the brain of the airplane, and he perceived only what it perceived, his eyes locked on the green light of radar display, the video-screen readout of his computer, and the display of lights and dials monitoring the aircraft's performance.

Flying sealed off like that might seem to rob combat aviation of its glamor. But Nick Brooks would not have agreed. He knew what he was doing. His quick reflexes and nimble mathematical mind followed the patterns of this super–space-war game. But this game was real. And the danger was real.

By rights Brooks should not have been on this mission—but he was one of the few navigators not sick with the flu in an epidemic that had spread on the USS *Ranger*. However, reasons were irrelevant. His hands flicked from knob to knob—star shaped, square, triangular, their different shapes telling different functions at a touch—while his eyes moved from screen to dial, to dial, to dial.

Their target appeared on the screen as a column of constantly changing figures. Brooks refined the data and transferred it to a simpler display so that Bruce Fryar, the pilot in the left-hand seat, could keep his eyes on the screen, the ground, and his wingman. The voice of the Forward Air Controller, high above them in an O2B, crackled in their ears.

Following the other aircraft, they made a low run down the line of trucks, released half their bomb load, and came off the deck to swing around for their final run. They were most vulnerable now.

The people on the ground—who were probably angry—knew they were up there, and they had defenses.

The lead aircraft made a wide loop to the right and came back in to drop the rest of its load. Brooks's plane followed it. . . .

Nick Brooks's entire right side was rocked by an explosion that thudded into him—not bad, only a nasty bruise, nothing broken. He straightened up. The computer had gone blank. . . .

"We're goin' in," Fryar shouted.

"Roger that." Brooks reached for the red handle. . . .

After U.S. Navy Lieutenant Commander Nicholas Brooks was shot down over Laos in 1970, his fate was unknown: Was he a prisoner, or had he been killed? Not until his body was returned to the United States in March 1982 did his parents' long, heartbreaking effort to discover his fate finally end. The record of their journey shows how the POW-MIA issue has been dealt with by our government and the reason why *Soldier of Fortune* supports every possible effort to bring back our men.

When Nick Brooks's plane went down in Laos in January 1970, the lives of his parents changed forever. Before, they had been an average middle-class American couple, who lived in New Windsor, New York, an upstate community, about nine miles from West Point, an almost perfect model for Norman Rockwell's America. George Brooks is a slender, compactly built man with a quick mind. His movements resemble those of a much younger man. Missing in action for two days himself, when his ship went down in the Mediterranean during WWII, he rose from seaman recruit to lieutenant, an engineering officer, during that war.

Nick's mother, Gladys, is a graceful woman, whose gray hair is one of the few clues that she is three times a grandmother. The Brookses have three children; they look like the archetypal American family. In fact, they are the best of what we all should be.

George Brooks wanted to stay in the Navy after WWII, but the long absences were hard on his family, so he took a job as an engineer with the Newburgh school system, and raised his kids. George and Gladys were proud when Nick sought and received an appointment to the Naval Academy, and then volunteered for destroyer duty off the Vietnamese coast. His parents were prouder still when the young man entered naval aviation as a navigator—although they would have preferred that their son not return for seconds in Vietnam.

Before Nick's plane went down, George and Gladys Brooks kept their eyes on the ball, their noses to the grindstone, their shoulders to the wheel, and a low profile. Since then, they have learned to walk the corridors of power in Washington and Paris, and have become familiar with the dusty streets of obscure Southeast Asian towns. They have become accomplished lobbyists. They have run a mom-and-pop intelligence agency out of their basement that has scooped the CIA, the Defense Intelligence Agency (DIA), and other obscure military intelligence units whose cover names are designed primarily to confuse.

If the efforts that the Brookses have put forth on what they call "The Issue" had been spent in their own behalf, they could have become rich. As it is, they plowed every cent they had ever saved, mortgaged their home, and borrowed against their insurance.

In a single year they have put $40,000 of their own money into "The Issue."

They are convinced that the Communist government has lied, that American prisoners are still being held in Vietnam and Laos. They, and others, have marshaled a credible body of evidence to that effect—but to get Congress and the DIA to acknowledge their evidence has been like swimming upstream against an avalanche of tapioca pudding.

Two questions immediately present themselves: Why would the Vietnamese keep these men after the end of hostilities? Why would our government not make every effort to get them back?

Thomas D. Boettcher and Joseph A. Rehyansky, in an article in the *National Review* of 21 August 1981, answer the first question. They conclude that the Vietnamese retain prisoners first for bargaining chips in future negotiations, and secondly, that it is Vietnamese policy not to release a prisoner until after he has cracked.

Boettcher and Rehyansky agree with Alexsandr Solzhenitsyn. Their article cites a 1975 speech in which the Russian compared the situation of American prisoners held by the government of North Vietnam to Solzhenitsyn's own experience in the Gulag Archipelago.

The Russian said, "There is a law in the Archipelago that those who have been treated the most harshly and who have withstood the most bravely, who are the most honest, the most courageous, the most unbending, never again come out into the world." The reason, Solzhenitsyn believes, is "because they will tell tales that the human mind can barely accept," tales of torture without yielding. These men, he declares, "are your best people. These are your foremost heroes who, in a solitary combat, have withstood the test. . . . They can't hear [our applause] from their solitary cells where they may either die or remain for thirty years."

It would be unfair to conclude that all released prisoners have compromised their integrity; this simply is not true. The communists are so squareheaded that it is easy to dazzle them with bullshit, obviously phony confessions, and satirical self-criticism sessions; all that goes right by them. What is true, however, is that an American POW who tried to adhere rigidly to the pre-Vietnam Code of Conduct would probably rot in prison.

The second question, why our government has forgotten these men, is harder to answer. Here reason becomes even murkier. We were able to unearth only one government document that addresses this issue with any candor. It is a 1974 memo to the Senate Foreign Relations Committee, from Senate Aide Dick Moose. Its headline reads: FOR COMMITTEE USE ONLY: NOT FOR PUBLICATION.

Copies of this memo were placed on the large table around which the POW-MIA issue was being discussed, before the chair of each committee member. A member of the National League of Families was invited to sit in the chair reserved for an absent senator. When he seated himself he saw the memo. He immediately swept it into his briefcase.

The memo declares that many of the relatives of the missing know there is little chance of finding survivors or obtaining information from the North Vietnamese but are reluctant to accept these facts. Furthermore, the memo says, "Officials with whom the families meet are equally reluctant to speak frankly with them. Instead the families are continuously reassured—out of compassion and probably political caution as well—that every effort will continue to be made to obtain an accounting for the missing." These reassurances, the memo asserts, serve only to keep up hope and family efforts to obtain government action.

The memo declares in a section headlined "Areas of Particular Sensitivity": "The families are upset by statements to the effect that all our prisoners have been returned. The Pentagon still carries more than fifty men on its rolls as POWs." It also declares that in many cases "there have been North Vietnamese press photographs or broadcasts involving specific prisoners who have never been accounted for.

"The possibility of additional prisoners in Laos is a major item of interest. The administration has said that we hold the DRV responsible under the Paris Accords for POWs throughout Indochina, but only nine of more than three hundred listed as missing in Laos were returned. The United States is not a party to the Lao settlements and it is now apparent that we are dependent on the Pathet Lao [Lao Patriotic Front] for further information in that area."

As to other possible actions, the memo declares that no one agrees about what further action could be taken. Many families want the United States to generate more worldwide publicity about the MIAs. They want statements by high government officials, Congress, USIA, and VOA. They want the United States to raise the MIA issue in the UN and other international forums. Others want complete trade and communication embargoes against North Vietnam. A few even, the memo continues, "urge military action but others recognize that this would lead to more casualties and that, in any event, it is not politically feasible."

Anyone with a military background has difficulty understanding how it can be "politically feasible" to allow the lives of some of our finest young men to be thrown away like used Kleenex. Former POWs and officers still on active duty who have tried to speak out on this matter have been squelched. Some, like Colonel Laird Gutterson, of Phoenix,

Arizona, have been forced into early retirement: Gutterson wouldn't keep quiet although he was told that delicate negotiations were under way, and unauthorized public statements would jeopardize them. In other words, patriotic, public-spirited officers should keep their mouths shut and not make waves. That was in 1973.

So far the "delicate negotiations" have yielded nothing.

The statistics in Moose's memo to the Foreign Relations Committee demonstrate conclusively that men were captured, alive and walking, by the North Vietnamese and Laotians. Either they were murdered in captivity, allowed to die from mistreatment—or they are still being held.

Whatever their fate, the fighting men of America, and their families, must demand an accounting.

Congress should not lose sight of the fact that, as far as we can determine, every man who is missing is a regular—either a fighter-bomber jock or a SOG reconnaissance trooper. The professional military has always been something of an institution apart in this country. It's not a large constituency, nor does it have ties to any specific voting bloc in Congress, outside, of course, the matter of appropriations. But a nation that breaks faith with its fighting men is a nation afflicted with suicidal tendencies.

Unfortunately, the search by families of missing men for facts and figures has been marred by broken promises and lack of cooperation. George Brooks cites the following episode to illustrate the length to which individual families have had to go to make even small corrections in the official records. "In 1974 the League of Families had a meeting in Omaha, Nebraska. Nick's squadron commander was stationed there. When we went out with him and his wife, he told us how Nick had been captured. He told us he had been tied to a tree, but had escaped and they caught him again and tied him to another tree.

"We said, 'Wait! Are you sure you're talking about Nick Brooks and Bruce Fryar [the pilot of Nick's airplane]?'

" 'Yes,' he said.

"We were surprised and happy to hear that. So next morning when the press came in after a board of directors meeting, and one reporter asked me, 'What's new?' I told him how happy my wife and I were to learn there was new information about Nick, because we hadn't been able to get it before. It meant a lot to us, learning our son was obviously in good physical condition, and he had to be if he could escape.

"The reporter printed this on the front page of the Omaha paper the next morning. Then we started catching flak. I was talking with Nick's squadron commander downstairs in the hotel, when I saw a Navy captain coming toward me with the newspaper scrunched up in his hand and fire in his eyes.

"I decided not to tell who had passed on the information to me. I figured I could get away with it, because Nick's squadron commander was in civilian clothes.

"But they had been classmates at the Academy. So they went round and round. 'Did you tell this man this? How come?'

" 'Because it's true,' Nick's squadron commander answered. 'I saw the report on board ship.'

" 'Well, there isn't any such report,' the captain said.

"It was hard to deal with. But they did promise that they'd go back to Washington, search for that report, and put it in Nick's record. That was in July. We waited until January 1975. At that time Gladys asked for an appointment with the secretary of the Navy."

Mrs. Brooks nodded. "The Pentagon called me here and confirmed the appointment. In the meantime the anniversary of the ceasefire, twenty-seven January, was coming up—when the League of Families normally held a candlelight vigil at the White House. We decided to tie the vigil in with our appointment. When we got to Washington, we called our youngest son, Richard, at home. He said,

'Mom, a letter came for you from the Navy Department in the mail this afternoon.'

"I said, 'Open it up and read it to me.' The letter told me—after confirmation of my appointment by telephone—that the secretary of the Navy was too busy to meet with me, but that Assistant Secretary McCollum would.

"Well, I decided right then and there that I had never received the letter. Because we knew how these things work, we stopped by the office of Ben Gilman, our congressman. I told him I had a meeting with the Navy secretary, and asked if he had time to sit in on it with me.

"He said, 'Sure.'

"We agreed to meet at the Pentagon. When I walked in, I saw a large table and the brass seated all around it. There were at least twelve men, including Roger Shields, the Deputy Secretary of defense. Mr. McCollum stood up.

"He came up to me and said, 'Mrs. Brooks, I'm sorry that Navy Secretary Menninger cannot meet with you.'

"I had my act together. I screamed. I forgot I was a lady. I told them how upset I was. McCollum tried to calm me. Soon Representative Gilman walked in. Then there was a lot of scurrying around.

"During the confusion of greeting the congressman and introducing him around, I didn't see who left the room, but within seconds the secretary of the Navy appeared. He had time for a congressman.

"As a result of that meeting we got a deposition from Nick's squadron commander and this information was included in Nick's file. Everything that we have gotten has been like pulling teeth. They would never have included the information we discovered in Omaha in Nick's file if it hadn't been for my asking our congressman to come to the meeting."

I don't suppose that anyone who has ever been in the service will be surprised that bureaucracy moves only when it is pushed. But the Brookses are extraordinary, tenacious people. They will not be denied.

Before the truce the League of Families was a valuable propaganda tool for the government. Red carpets were rolled out everywhere. George Brooks explained, "I was meeting on a regular basis with Henry Kissinger. We could get telephone calls answered no matter where. Before the truce we had tremendous cooperation. Donations for the League came in as fast as we could use them, from prime government contractors, Grumman Aircraft and people like that. The families didn't have to contribute a penny.

"But the POW issue was being used to justify the continuation of the war. That was during the Nixon administration. The president even came to a National League of Families meeting. After Nixon it took a while to realize we'd been completely cut off by the government, which was now saying, 'Let's forget it.'

"A lot of other families were working hard also," Brooks went on. "Some of them have become disillusioned. I can't fault them, after all those broken promises. Henry Kissinger said all our men would be accounted for in the same time frame as the withdrawal of our troops from Vietnam. That included the time up until Saigon's fall in 1975.

"When the troops were withdrawn, there was no accounting whatsoever. The families saw the promises, made to them over a long period of time, go down the drain, and many said, 'It's useless. We can't do any more.'

"But some continued. We held rallies at the White House and the United Nations, sent Gladys's newsletter to people, and encouraged people to hang in."

Despite their disillusionment with the government the Brookses are quick to credit the many people within it who have gone to extraordinary lengths to keep the POW-MIA issue alive, often at some risk to their own careers.

PFOD—presumptive finding of death—is one obstacle the families of the missing men come up against repeatedly, as well as the government's unwillingness to investigate reports of live sightings.

"We got a telephone call from a friend," Brooks said, "telling us that she had talked to a Vietnamese woman in New York City who said a refugee told her he had seen two Americans alive when he came out. We have never seen this Vietnamese woman, but we called her and asked her if we could talk to the man. She replied, 'Yes.'

"It is important to recognize that at the time this information was made available to us, it was also made available to the DIA. But they absolutely refused to talk about it. They admitted that they didn't know if the story were true or false, and yet they wouldn't bring this guy in and run him on the box [lie detector].

"I then talked to a returned POW, a Colonel Ray. He said, 'Gee, George, maybe I can help you. I've got a friend who's a licensed polygrapher.' Ray's wife and I got the refugee a motel room in Montgomeryville, Pennsylvania. They put the guy on the box. It took several hours. I had gotten an interpreter who has a doctorate from the University of Pittsburgh, a man who came here from Vietnam to study. It was the judgment of everybody involved with the polygraph test that, yes, this man was telling the truth. Even then the DIA wouldn't check it out.

"Meanwhile, we had started to run ads in Vietnamese-language magazines. Reports started to come in from all over the world. After we collected a lot of these reports, we decided that the government must have some, too. So in February 1978, we asked them for whatever reports they had under the Freedom of Information Act.

"The reports were delivered in July of that year. We looked through them and decided there was a lot of information that should be known. Gladys and I sat down and meticulously analyzed each one. There were 318 in one batch and 271 in the second."

Brooks paused. He said, "It's an interesting sidelight—

not one of those refugees asked us for anything. They could have asked for anything they wanted."

Then he returned to the main point. "We looked to see what action had been taken on the reports. Nothing had been done with those that they had had for some time. Not only had nothing been done with them, but worse yet, they didn't intend to do anything. A sizable number were first-hand reports of live sightings. Our government was totally disinterested. At the time, August '78, we were under terrific pressure because of the congressional delegation that was going to Hanoi. It was headed by Representative Lester Wolff, then chairman of the Asian and Pacific Affairs Committee in Congress. We wanted to have an analysis of the reports ready for the delegation. I read every one of those cotton-picking reports, right on through.

"We got the analysis delivered to the plane that was taking the congressmen to Hanoi. We learned later that copies of our report with the analysis were given to General Eugene Tighe, who was then director of the Defense Intelligence Agency. I would like to believe that he was disturbed because it showed there were American servicemen still over there. I think, more realistically, he was disturbed because he saw an indictment of his own organization.

"For that reason he decided they should do something. They invited me down. A number of refugees have now been submitted to polygraphic examinations, but until our reports were published, the government wouldn't talk to these people.

"Admiral Jerry Tuttle, a highly respected Navy officer, who had been commanding officer of the USS *Kennedy*, will admit frankly that when he was assigned to investigate the POW-MIA issue, he thought that all our guys were back. The people in the Defense Department thought the whole thing was over. The government had done a hell of a good job of saying that we got everybody back.

"Then things began to turn around, as Tuttle learned

what was really happening. He brought in Pat Hurt, one of his own investigators. The more Tuttle got into it, the more excited he became. He got so involved that when he was lunching with other officers in the Pentagon, he would bring up the subject of American prisoners in Vietnam.

"Then came the Carter administration. We have documents of all his campaign promises: The POWs won't be abandoned; Vietnam will not get a seat in the United Nations until an accounting has been made. When he got in office, he broke these promises.

"Although we weren't Carter supporters, I thought he might be helpful, because his uncle, a Navy enlisted man, had been captured in WWII in the South Pacific. He was listed as MIA. About two years later he was listed as MIA. His wife remarried. After we won the war, he was found in an isolated prison camp in Japan, emaciated, but alive. That's a traumatic thing to happen in your own family. We hoped that Jimmy Carter would recognize what happens in a family if a man is declared dead without evidence."

Largely because of the Brooks's efforts, the DIA is now actively seeking live-sighting reports from Vietnamese refugees. From 26 in 1977, the year before the reports were correlated, these sightings climbed to 75 in 1978, and 448 in 1979.

Curiously enough, however, now that the Brookses have got the DIA actively involved in the POW-MIA issue, it has classified all subsequent reports as secret; the Brookses no longer have access to them. They do, however, continue to turn over to the DIA all reports that they get through Vietnamese-language magazines.

The Brookses were not particularly pleased with the Reagan administration, pointing out that Soviet dissidents have received more public support than have the American POWs. But there is evidence that the Reagan administration took the POW-MIA issue seriously: increased live-sighting reports, more aerial reconnaissance flights, and U.S. government-backed forays into Laos.

In 1981 the Brookses invested in a plan to send a private force of ex-SOG troopers into Laos for information—or for the men themselves if they could be found and freed. That project flopped due to errors in planning and premature publicity, but others, less publicized, are ongoing.

At dinner I watched closely this couple I had come to know and like. Their love is obvious. They smiled at each other when I was looking, and winked when they thought I wasn't. They are not above holding hands in public. On the way back to my hotel George told me, "You know, Gladys and I haven't had a vacation in twelve years. We'd like to take a trip west in a Winnebago, see some of the country."

George was tired when he said that to me in November 1981. Maybe he meant it at the time and maybe not. But he has not slackened his interest in the POW-MIA issues, although his son's body was returned to the United States early in 1982 under interesting and suspicious circumstances.

In March of that year Nick Brooks's remains were brought to the U.S. embassy in Bangkok by some members of the Lao resistance. They wanted $2,500 for the bones, which the embassy refused to pay, in accord with its policy of not buying bodies. No one knows why or how, but later the remains were brought to the embassy by former Laotian General Phoumi Nosavan. The U.S. Army's Central Identification Laboratory in Hawaii identified the bones as those of Nick Brooks.

George is not inherently suspicious, but he had the family dentist check Nick's records: These are indeed Nick's remains.

Several questions emerge from this brief summary. Was it sheer coincidence that the remains of the son of the most active troublemaker of the League of Families were returned? Or do the Lao or Vietnamese have hundreds of bodies stored and collated for use in God knows what scheme? And did they think they could shut George and Gladys Brooks up by returning their son's body to America?

If that was their strategy, it didn't work. George is now the chairman of the National League of Families. Gladys still puts out her newsletter. "When we banded together with the League," says George, "we fought for all the men, not just our son."

The first major event of 1983 for George Brooks and the League came at the end of January. President Reagan spoke to the League on 27 January, the tenth anniversary of the Vietnamese ceasefire that was supposed to bring all of the POWs home and account for the MIAs.

Ten years—that's a long time.

Lieutenant Commander Nicholas G. Brooks was buried with full military honors at Arlington Cemetery on 25 March 1982.

# Bones

Through the slatted windows of Colonel Y's house in U Dorn, I saw his pickup pull in through the gate and drive under his carport. Three short brown men, solid as fire-plugs, minor leaders of the Lao Resistance, got out and walked to the door.

Since the fall of Saigon the Vietnamese had assumed control of Laos and Cambodia, through puppet governments. The Cambodians had three fairly well-organized resistance factions fighting the Viets, but the Lao had hundreds; every squad leader was his own general. They were no threat to the central government, but, hidden in the jungle as they were, that government was little threat to them either.

Our host, Colonel Y, a retired Royal Thai Army officer who had fought in Laos, got up and opened the door. He was a short man, even for a Thai, who moved with the controlled grace of the boxer he had been, his heavily mus-cled shoulders swaying as he walked. Everything but his close-cropped gray hair belied his sixty-two years. He reminded me of James Cagney. Colonel Y opened the door and the three Lao entered shyly, ducking their heads. They pressed their palms together and bowed, one after the other.

General Heinie Aderholt, Tom Reisinger, and I rose and

returned the bow. Heinie was Air Force, our only high-school-dropout general. He had retired as a colonel, after running all air ops for the CIA for seven years, then been brought back on active duty as a brigadier when one of his former protégés became an assistant secretary of defense. After one tour as the senior U.S. armed forces officer in Thailand, he had retired again.

Reisinger was a former Special Forces medic, a stocky, handsome man with wavy, prematurely gray hair. Normally, since Bob Brown, our publisher, was too free with his enthusiasms to be let loose with a checkbook, he traveled with Brown and held the money. But Brown hadn't arrived in Thailand yet.

Tom and I shifted to other chairs, so the Lao could talk to General Aderholt, with Colonel Y acting as interpreter.

In the three days we had been in Thailand we had talked to half a dozen people who claimed to know where there were live POWs in Laos. If all these people were telling the truth, then we'd have to form them up in squadron formation and march them out in a column of fours. But a couple of our informants had seemed possibly reliable.

Those we gave fingerprint cards and sent back in. But, even assuming there were live POWs in Laos, we were told that publicity over Bo Gritz's abortive mission, in which he and several other Americans had gone across the river and patrolled for them themselves, and Agency-backed forays by Laotian nationals, had caused the POWs to be moved back a long way from the border. It was a three-month walk in and out with those fingerprint cards.

Our most knowledgeable and reliable source claimed to know of a camp where thirty-two American POWs were held, almost on the Lao-Vietnamese border. He said they were kept in individual holes in the ground, widely separated, and guarded by a six-hundred-man Vietnamese special unit. If this was so, then they knew that we knew, and had chosen these measures to prevent a rescue attempt.

Recent tentative Vietnamese initiatives, the trip to Hanoi by the VVA Four, representatives of a Vietnam Veterans group that has little credibility among most Vietnam vets, a trip by Deputy Defense Secretary Richard Armitage, were part of a Vietnamese attempt to use our POWs as their strongest bargaining card for diplomatic recognition, and for what they would call reparations and I would call extortion.

But if the Oriental mind seems inscrutable to us, the Viets, still, after all these years, had no frame of reference for a cast of mind as unsubtle or impatient as the Americans'. They searched the U.S. government's most sincere overtures for hidden meanings that weren't there, simultaneously wondering why the long-noses couldn't take a hint.

At first our only lead was the cadaver—"cadiver," Heinie called it—across the Mekong River from Nakan Phanom, which led us to this meeting in U Dorn.

Heinie and Colonel Y sat in chairs at either end of the coffee table and the three Lao sat in a row on the couch, smiling shyly, sipping tea brought by the colonel's lovely, sarong-clad young wife, his fifth, concurrent.

"We no have all body," said the Lao who spoke English. "When we come back, Vietnamee attack us. We have two men get kill."

"What bone you have?" Heinie insisted.

The two Lao gave him a stupefied look, and then nodded as Colonel Y translated the question. They conferred among themselves in a language that sounded like the symptoms of an upper respiratory disorder.

"We have two leg bone, one arm bone, part of head bone."

"What you want?" Heinie addressed the question to Colonel Y, who translated quite pointedly in Lao.

They proposed a strange bargaining scheme by which we would pay what we thought it was worth, and if they liked the deal they'd bring us more bodies. We weren't very happy with that, but agreed, and made a deal to go pick the bones up in the colonel's truck at first light the following morning.

The next day, twenty miles down the road toward Nakon Phanom, our driver, a young man named Prek, braked to a halt in front of a large refugee center, which held tens of thousands of Lao who had not been accepted for immigration by any nation. The Thais did not want them, but they weren't losing money on the deal; the U.S., primarily, paid for the refugee centers. But we didn't want the refugees in the States, either, in spite of being the richest, and one of the least populated, nations in the western world. Since America was viewed as the author of this exile, other nations felt no moral obligation to step in.

The refugee center was a series of low green buildings, more like barracks than anything else. Two of the Lao we had met the day before, another man, and a Lao girl in a sarong and blouse gingerly climbed into the back of the pickup, where Tom and Heinie sat in two rattan armchairs from Colonel Y's living room.

I didn't know who the other guy and the girl were, and while the Lao who spoke English was along, the one who was in charge, and who had seemed the most intelligent, was not. There was a strong possibility we were being jerked around. I didn't like it.

Apparently neither did General Aderholt. He jumped into the face of the English-speaking Lao like a drill instructor. In a few moments, though, he appeared satisfied, and we roared off down the road.

The road was a good, solid, two-lane blacktop. Heinie had said that five years before there had been no such road in northeast Thailand. They had all been dirt roads then, and you couldn't drive on them without being shot at.

Not only had the Thais succeeded against their insurgency without American troops, they actually did better after we pulled our advisors out. Nonetheless, our help had been crucial for a time; they succeeded with techniques learned from U.S. Army Special Forces.

Fair enough. The Chinese-backed Thai insurgents and Special Forces both had taken their techniques from Mao. The Royal Thai SF just used them better.

This was a good road, and, oh, how the Thais loved it. So much so that, in addition to a road, they used it as a sidewalk, a bike lane, and a buffalo crossing.

On either side we passed graceful wooden houses, high on pilings, set among palms, coconut, and papaya, jackfruit and banana trees, paddies and buffalo wallows, bougain-villaea, and flame-of-the-forest trees.

We snapped around entire families on spitting motorcy-cles, three-wheel Japanese trucks decorated with chromed representations of Thai mythology, flocks of kids in school uniforms on bicycles, all over the highway, who paid little or no attention to the ton or so of moving steel bearing down on them.

I glanced over at Prek, who stared straight down the road with a look of grim determination, his right foot firmly mashing the accelerator to the floor.

I leaned over to read the speedometer. The needle wa-vered around 135. "Holy shit!" I muttered before realizing it read in kilometers. That's still somewhere between 85 and 90 miles an hour. One of the little girls unconcernedly leaned her bicycle out of our path just before Prek swerved to miss a water buffalo cow, nursing her calf astride the centerline.

We were in that truck for seven hours that day, and Prek spent the entire time with either the accelerator or the brake jammed to the floor.

I twisted to look back in the bed of the truck. Heinie sat with his feet propped up on his suitcase, trying to read about El Salvador in the rice-paper Far East edition of *New-sweek*. I turned around in time to see a line of three water

buffalo amble in a leisurely fashion across the road. It occurred to me that here and in Lebanon I had experienced
more danger from traffic than from the guns of the enemy.

A few minutes later Heinie pounded on the rear window.
I turned and he shouted something. "What?" I bellowed
back. This time I caught it. "Mekong!" he bellowed.

Through the vegetation I caught a glimpse of a broad,
brown expanse of water, the spooky green gnarled karst
mountains of Laos jumping up through haze on the other
side. The last time I had seen that river was in Phnom Penn
nine years before, when I went swimming with some happy
kids, who had since probably been executed.

An hour later we rolled into Nakon Phanom and dropped
off the Lao resistance leaders and their entourage, with a
prearranged time and place to meet.

For the next hour and a half we prowled the streets of
NKP, looking at jewelry and rattan.

For lunch we ate Chinese noodles at a shanty restaurant
overlooking the red-brown river, wide as two football
fields, prowled by sampans, and beyond that about ten
miles of flat lush delta, past which the mountains made their
weird appearance. A few hundred meters downriver were
a pier and a Pathet Lao customhouse. I strained to see a
PL, or possibly a Vietnamese weapons position, but at that
time of day there was not likely to be a person vertical in
Laos.

Mekong Delta soil is among the world's richest, and
everyone on this side was well fed, clothed, and housed,
saving to buy a motorbike if they didn't already have one.
Yet, when Heinie asked what it was like in Laos, the Chinese lady who owned this restaurant said there was "no rice
on the other side."

We sipped cold Coke through straws, while the radio
played Beatles songs.

Heinie sang along. "Let it be, let it be, let it be, let it

be-ee-ee," although he seemed like the last man in the
world to follow that advice.

We made our pickup on time and drove to an isolated spot
out along the river to make the exchange.

The bones were wrapped in a dusty gunnysack, with
some dirt clods, inside a yellow plastic bag. For all I could
see, the bone that Tom identified as the femur could have
been any long bone from any kind of animal, but even to
the untrained eye there was very little else the skullcap
could have been but a skullcap. Heinie gave the Lao one
thousand baht, which is about forty bucks U.S., to buy a
couple of bags of rice for their families, with the promise
of much more than that if the remains proved to be Cau-
casian. Then we piled in the truck for another screaming
ride to catch our plane for Bangkok.

"There is no joy in this business," said Air Force Lieutenant
Colonel Paul Mather, a bespectacled, scholarly looking man
who ran the office of the Joint Casualty Resolution Center
at our embassy in Bangkok, "but we have helped alleviate
the misery of some POW families, and that's no small
thing." We spent several hours with him, discussing pros-
pects for the acquisition of more remains. The embassy's
position was that they would not pay for remains of people
who had died defending the freedom of those who were
trying to blackmail us now.

This is an understandable and defensible position. But it
is also understandably not shared by families of the downed
pilots, who have, on occasion, been taken for huge sums
of money for buffalo bones.

Heinie was trying to bring a more effective approach to
this by paying the Laotians an adequate amount to recom-
pense them for their time and the danger they have braved
to help us, but only for the real thing.

Colonel Mather seemed pleased with our contribution.

The remains were to be transported under full military escort to Hawaii for forensic evaluation. The skullcap would be compared with ID photos of the men who had flown the aircraft that matched the tail number we got from the Laotians. These remains would be flown under the normal military escort given to American dead, and if they checked out, which they did, would finally be buried with the respect due the body of a man who had given his life for his country, and for the freedom of others, so long ago and so very far away.

# Singlaub's POW Rescue Mission

In WW II the POW situation was handled much differently, because, for the most part, we knew who and where they were, and after it was over we occupied the territory. Even so, POW rescue was difficult. Now retired, Major General John K. Singlaub led one such operation as a young captain with the OSS. Here is his story of his experiences in Southeast Asia, culminating in that mission.

We arrived in India in the upper Assam valley and discovered that it was going to take several weeks before our priority would allow us to fly over the hump into China.

Colonel Peers, commander of Detachment 101 (later commanding general of the 4th Division in Vietnam, and chairman of the Peers Commission to investigate the My Lai massacre) was moving some of his assets from a place called Dinjan in the upper Assam Valley, up to Bhamo in Burma. So I volunteered to run a series of convoys up the Burma Road to occupy my guys while we were waiting to get over the hump. So we took that on, and drove the Ledo road up to Bhamo.

And then, strangely enough, we flew back from Bhamo to Chabua and then flew on over the hump to Kunming.

When we got to Kunming, my radio operator from

France wanted to stay with me, so I still had him. I did some Chinese language training, and then went down to Poseh and trained some Chinese guerrillas for operations against the Japanese.

By this time I had my team; we had a weapons man, a medic and my radio operator, and an executive officer, all Americans. We were to take a team into what is now called North Vietnam, but was then Indochina. My mission was to blow the railroad and a road between Hanoi and the town of Langson. The road and the railroad were on opposite sides of this gorge.

It was a very deep gorge, and the railroad was an easy one to cut, because it had a lot of curved rails, and it had a limited number of culverts. The road was more difficult, but again it was on a—in several places—on a very steep gorge, and it had culverts, which I was able to spot and compute my charges. And I found out where my drop zone was going to be. We were to take in some Vietnamese with us when we went.

When I went on reconnaissance flights in a C-47, to check my targets, my drop zone and so on, I carried along supplies to drop to the team that was advising Ho Chi Minh, so I would fly over Ho Chi Minh's headquarters at a place called Tuyen Guang.

Ho had a lot of charisma, and ability to get people to work with him, and continued to promise that they were going to attack the Japanese. They didn't do as much attacking of the Japanese as we would have liked. But at that time the Vietnamese that I worked with—they had run intelligence nets—said that they recognized the need for continuing help from the West, and they expected the French to return.

They wanted to be able to teach Vietnamese in their schools, and they wanted some concessions from their colonial rulers, but they did not want to give up contact with the West. They said they would prefer that the Americans would come in and take over that role, but recognized that was not likely.

But they did not have that absolute hatred, that intransigent position that they later took. That's a long story, a very complicated and involved story, how that developed.

I never executed that mission.

We were all set to go. Then down in this little jungle town we had people come in and say that a big bomb had been dropped on Japan, and the war was going to be over.

Aw, get outa here! We didn't know what they were talking about. Then eventually we were told that our mission was canceled, and they were sending a plane to pick me up.

A day or so later a plane came in and flew us back to Kunming. And then we were told, "The States has dropped an atom bomb on Japan, and we think they're going to surrender in the very near future. Our current problem is that the Japanese hold an awful lot of prisoners in various places. We want to send some teams in to get those prisoners before the Japanese execute them, because they've treated them so badly that they may think it's safer just to kill them all, than let them tell how badly they were treated."

So they asked if I would volunteer to lead a team to go into Hainan Island, where they thought there were some prisoners. There were other teams being brought back from other parts of China, where they had been fighting against the Japanese. One was sent to Formosa—Taiwan—teams were sent to Mukden, Peking, Shantung, Shanghai, Korea.

I elected to jump my force because we didn't have an airfield. But the team that went to Taiwan, the Japanese just put a pistol to their face, and said get back on the airplane.

I recruited my team—took some of my former team members and added to them. In the two days I had to get ready for this an important part of our preparation was to analyze photos and try to see where the camp was. I was finally convinced of the exact building, and selected a drop zone. So we flew from Kunming one night, over the Gulf of Tonkin, right on the deck, just fifty feet off the ocean, made landfall—I recognized it from the studies—turned right, went in, and picked out the exact spot.

I picked out my heading, and told the pilot to let us out at six hundred feet. So we parachuted into this area, which was within sight of the buildings where we thought the POWs were. The aircraft was supposed to make another pass and drop our equipment, but . . . I don't know if he was trying to get lower and look and see if we were all right, but he dropped at too low an altitude for the parachutes to open.

So my radio was about two meters wide by fifty meters long. The bundle just exploded, and ruined a lot of the other supplies we were taking in.

So we were without a radio. And, of course, the Japanese there had not been told that the war was over at all.

At that time, about the beginning of August, the Japanese government had indicated that they were ready to surrender. But the people on this island—there were about ten thousand Japanese on the island, big guys, Hokkaido Marines—had been winning all their battles. So they weren't very kind to us for the first thirty-six hours.

They policed us up and put us in a guardhouse. But I wouldn't talk to the captain commanding it.

I was a captain, but for that jump the intelligence people convinced my team and me that I should wear major's leaves. So I was a brevet major.

This was a good thing, because there is such a big distinction between company and field grade officers in the Japanese army. I hadn't understood that, but the intelligence officer did. So as a major I wouldn't deign to speak to this captain. I said I wanted to talk to his colonel.

We heard the captain on his telephone, because he had to yell so loud. I had a nisei and a Chinese with me as interpreters, as part of the nine-man force. The captain said, "But, Colonel, he won't talk to me. He insists on talking to you. The major insists on talking to you.

"But, Colonel, he insists that Japan is going to surrender!

"But, Colonel, they jumped in broad daylight!" We could only hear one end of the conversation, but we could tell roughly what it was.

So I had a very, very nervous night, without any communications, in fact, locked up in the guardhouse. I had insisted that I wanted to see the commander of the allied prisoners, and that I wanted to see the colonel who was commanding this area.

Well, the next day they finally took us over to where I met with the Japanese. I told him that I absolutely insisted on seeing the allied officers in the camp.

He apparently had gotten the word by this time that the Japanese were about to surrender. So I told him that I was commandeering all the food on the island, and that, after allied needs were met, he would have the next priority. I was commandeering all the transportation, all the communications. And I wanted a liaison officer assigned to me immediately, but that the first order of business was to talk to the prisoners.

So they brought in an Australian colonel, the senior officer, and a Dutch lieutenant commander.

It was quite a reunion. Very emotional, as you can imagine. I moved the Japanese to the side, sat these guys down, after shaking their hands, and found out what their real problems were. Then I issued some ultimatums to the Japanese, as to what was going to be done specifically.

That operation, I suppose, was one of the most satisfying you could perform. Not only did we provide freedom to almost four hundred prisoners of war, but we had the job of bringing them up to date on what had happened since they had been captured. They had been captured by the Japanese very early in the Pacific war in February of 1942, on a small island in what is now Indonesia. At that time it was the Netherlands East Indies.

They had been very badly treated by the Japanese. They had been physically abused. They had been put on the most inhospitable part of the island, and when the monsoons hit there the water would not only come through the roof, but through the walls. They were dying several a day by the time I got there. So we were able to give them not only freedom, but by feeding them six small meals a day, we stopped the deaths by starvation. And we gave them vitamin B-1 injections, and provided them with some essential medical care, although some died still, after we got there.

Intelligence nets that I set up initially indicated that there had been some Americans that had been captured, and had been killed by the Japanese.

We found evidence of this. One of the things given to me on my first entry into the camp was a packet of documentation of atrocities committed against these people. That evidence, which I held on to until I personally turned it over to the British authorities in Hong Kong, was used to try some of the Japanese for war crimes after the war.

I had great pressure from the Japanese; they wanted to surrender to me. They did not want to wait and surrender to the Chinese. But it was very clear in my instructions that I would not accept their surrender, and the Japanese just could not understand. They wanted to come and present their swords to me rather than face surrender to the Chinese, whom they had not treated particularly well in the course of that war, as we all know.

Then I had the problem of moving the former prisoners from that location on the west side of the island down to the southern tip, where there was an adequate harbor and an airfield. I commandeered a train and was moving them down there when our train was ambushed and the engine was derailed. The rail was blown, but we were flying a homemade American flag on the train. The blue field was denim and the stripes were sheets, with the wrong number of stars and the wrong number of stripes.

But that train was never assaulted. That's a good thing, because I only had four armed Americans on it. The rest were unarmed prisoners. We never did find out whether that ambush was the work of bandits or guerrillas.

So we had to go through all of that to get 'em down there. Some of them weren't up to rail travel, so we had to move them by boat down to the other end of the island, where I preceded to set up better hospital facilities.

It was a better part of the island. There was fresh fruit available for them there. We took over some barracks that had belonged to the Japanese Air Force and made it into a hospital and barracks for the troops, until I could eventually bring in some Australian ships to evacuate the Australians and the Dutch up to Hong Kong.

I found that there were some prisoners who had escaped and were presumed to be inside the island, and some in the interior.

I had the problem of locating where these escapees and evaders were. So I eventually got the airfield repaired in the south, and brought in, asked for . . . Well, first of all I had the problem of not having any radio.

We'd had some signals, though, that we had been able to display on the drop zone. It was agreed that twenty-four hours after our drop, they would send a reconnaisance flight over the drop zone and photograph it. I had a series of signals to display by spreading out the reserve parachutes, which were white, in different patterns.

Fortunately I was able to get my people, two guys, out of that guardhouse where we were, and out to the drop zone to display that signal on the second day. First day our plane went over and there was nothing, so they were quite worried in Kunming. Second day I was able to indicate that we were out of communication, but we were okay. If we had been under duress, we had a way of mutilating the panel display slightly, so that they would have known it.

It wasn't until I got down to the southern end of the island that we took over a big Japanese transmitter, and sent back a message to Kunming telling what had happened and where we were.

When we boomed in with that big signal from the Japanese transmitter, they wouldn't believe it was us, so we had to go through a lot of challenges to prove we were, in fact, who we said we were. I was then able to bring in a doctor on a plane.

And I was able to use that plane to fly over the island. I threw in small bottles of Atabrine tablets. I was able to use small parachutes from our jump, the pilot chutes, to float things down. I threw messages into large villages that said, "Take this to your leader. The allies have landed a small force on the southern part of the island. The Japanese are surrendering. The war is over. We want to make contact with any allied former prisoners or evaders, any allied personnel, and send a message to a given place, the southern part of the island, town of Sanya."

Two days later we got a message that came in answer to that, one signed by an Australian major, indicating that he had X number of Australian and Dutch troops with him, plus a large number of Indians who had escaped also. These were members of the Hong Kong and Singapore Royal Artillery. They were Sikhs.

The Japanese had tried to form a Free India movement. But these people, when given an opportunity to serve the Japanese, had headed for the hills. There were also some Americans.

Several messages came in. One of them was signed by the Australian major, and another was from an American who was an evader in the interior of the island.

So I had getting in there as part of my problem of getting around. The only way I could get to my rear detachment was to parachute in.

That's when I made my first free-fall. I used one of the emergency parachutes from this airplane—one of the airplanes that flew in supplies. I took the reserve that was still intact and cut the old harness that I had jumped in with, tied knots in the risers above the connectors, so that I had a harness for my reserve, and then did a free-fall out of a C47.

I had no idea how much altitude I should allow, but I decided I would need five seconds to clear the airplane, and pull the thing, so I computed this on the basis of the velocity of a free-falling body, and jumped from less than a thousand feet.

When I got into free-falling, later on, I realized how silly that was. But anyway it was successful, and I got back in there.

Eventually we had to go back into the interior of the island, and that was an exciting thing because the Japanese controlled the perimeter of the island, in most cases, and then in the interior you had three separate groups; you had procommunist guerrillas, and pro-Nationalist guerrillas, and then you had just plain bandits.

I still don't know who it was that ambushed our train. It may have been just bandits, but in any case you had to go through several territories. The Japanese would only take us so far, and then they said, "Well, down that road there"— they called them all bandits—"there are some bandits," and we'd go down and cautiously display an American flag. Then that group would take us to the end of the area they controlled, and eventually we got in. We made arrangements to come out a few days later. So we brought out several truckloads of escapers and evaders.

I must say the Chinese Nationalist commander on the island gave us one of the finest Chinese meals I've ever had, in celebration of this great occasion. It was a twenty-six course dinner, as I recall.

We evacuated the majority of the prisoners via destroyer.

I went out with one of the first groups of destroyers to get a hospital ship to come in and pick up the ones who were really in bad shape. By that time a group of logisticians from the China headquarters came in and relieved me. They were from the services of supply. They had the responsibility of staying there until the Chinese army came.

I flew then with the team to Hong Kong. We happened to be there the night of the official surrender signing. By this time the majority of the ships of the British navy had assembled in Hong Kong and they put on quite a fireworks display that night. That was about the second of September, I think, in '45.

A few days later we flew back to Kunming and I released the team.

# VETERANS

# Dojo Life

On the avenue, Fifth Avenue, and I'm steppin' right out in my Bally loafers, my Ralph Lauren trousers, my Armani jacket, my Valentino tie, my haircut that cost just over fifty bucks, including tip. So, naturally I take a self-satisfied glance in a passing store window. No question, the clothes look great. I, on the other hand, look old, tired, and soft. My gut billows, my ass protrudes, my big flat feet flop on my ankles like a marionette's feet with the strings cut.

Later in the men's room at the office I notice my jowls sag, and there are huge bags behind my glasses.

After a ten-year career pull I am a success; I am also about six months shy of a heart attack.

These past six years in New York an average work-week had been eighty to a hundred hours. It had worked. I had become one of the people I envied, and I now envied a higher level of sharpers and highbinders. But I could not say, as I had for this level, that I was going to become one of those people if it killed me, because there was no doubt that it would.

What to do, what to do? I couldn't run; my left leg is two inches shorter than the right from a parachuting accident, and if I run on concrete, walking after is a painful hobble. My study was clogged with ignored exercise equipment. Not even the will to survive can keep me on a rowing machine for long.

I started thinking of a return to the martial arts. I had started judo in college, then again in the army, but dropped out after a dislocated shoulder. After the army I started aikido, loved the art, loved the people in it. Then I started moving, both up and around, and dropped out again.

Surely somewhere on the island of Manhattan there was an aikido dojo where I would feel at home.

I brought this problem up at lunch with a friend who used to write porn under the name Ed Charterman, and is now editor-in-chief at a major paperback house. Ed is a tall, skinny guy with a crazed glaze in his eye. Our friendship is based on a number of things, one of which is that we are the only action-adventure editors who have ever actually killed anybody. As a teenaged MP at Fort Bragg Ed blew away a rapist attempting unsuccessfully to flee the scene, and I spent a couple of years in the late sixties hosing down the jungle with an M16.

We were eating in a place called Bogie's, a mystery writer's hangout on West Twenty-third Street, dominated by a brooding Maltese Falcon, posters for Bogart movies, and autographed photos of famous mystery writers. "Ask Billy," he said. "He does that stuff."

Billy Palmer, who owns Bogie's, is a friendly, well-built little guy with an impressive walrus moustache. In addition to Bogie's he and his wife, Karen, package mysteries for paperback publishers, and run mystery parties and cruises where people act out mystery scenarios. I thought of him as one of those rare people who make a decent living having a good time. I waved him over, inspecting him closely in the light of this new knowledge.

Billy carried himself with an economy of movement. His stance was not aggressive, but balanced. He looks like neither a threat nor a target. He didn't seem like a tough guy;

he seemed self-contained. I have a notion that he is invisible to muggers.

He was, as it turned out, a fifth-degree black belt in jujitsu. "Billy, do you know of a Tomiki-style aikido dojo in New York?"

"Sure," he said. "Hundred and fifth and Riverside, at the American Buddhist Academy. Sensei's name is Higashi. He's the guy who brought the sport to the U.S."

Sensei? Oh, yeah, Japanese for teacher. I was in business.

I called Sensei Higashi and got the aikido schedule. The next afternoon I caught the uptown Number Two train. I had allowed plenty of time, so I got off the express at Ninety-sixth and walked through a mile of Riverside Park, strolling through the trees, and among people walking their dogs, joggers, kids playing catch. The setting sun cast a magenta sheen on the slimy water of the Hudson. Garbage scows and pleasure craft cut wakes on it. A police helicopter and an old WWI Wright biplane flew overhead, and I got the sense, which constantly recurs in New York, that I was trapped in a Ridley Scott movie.

At 104th I left the park and walked back up to Riverside. The American Buddhist Academy, which is actually a church, occupies an old mansion at 331 Riverside. Outside is a statue of Shinran Shonan, the founder of Jodo-Shinshu Buddhism. To my eye he looked like an old Okinawan fisherman. I had been stationed on Okinawa, and immediately felt at home in this place.

A pleasant-faced elderly Japanese man looked up from his seat as I entered. He smiled. "Very warm," he said.

"Yep," I replied. "Aikido?"

"Downstairs."

The stairs to the basement were narrow, dark, and steep. I groped my way down, wound through a short passageway, and came into the dojo proper. To the right was an area of tatami mats about fifty by a hundred feet. At the far end, high on the wall, were three eight-by-ten photos of luminaries, only one of whom I recognized, Dr. Jigaro Kano, the originator of judo. On the right-hand wall was a strange flag that incorporated the Japanese battle flag on top and a stylized Mount Fuji in blue on the bottom, with some Japanese writing. On the mat a class, formed up in two lines, went through a series of blocks and punches.

"That's not aikido," I said to one of three or four guys waiting at the edge of the mat; they wore white judo *gis*, and various colors of martial arts belts.

"Jujitsu," he replied.

Sensei Higashi glided across the mat in front of the class, watching the jujitsu people punch and kick their way through a kata. There seemed to be a seventy-to-thirty ratio of men to women, and age ranged down to about ten. One of the grown-ups got on his knees so his opponent, a ten-year-old with a higher belt than his own, would face a proper target.

Higashi, a stocky, stolid guy, stalked over and made small corrections on the boy's form. He moved with economy and grace as Billy had, only more so. His manner was thorough, but kindly and gentle, a good-hearted man. He wore an old belt around his *gi,* alternating vertical bands of red and white at six-inch intervals. I had no idea what the belt signified, some area of mastery beyond my ken.

After a while Sensei called out, "Line up," and the jujitsu people formed up in one rank of white-clad soldiers. There were shouted commands from the senior black belt, a short ceremony that involved sitting on one's heels, Japanese style, bowing, and shouting something in Japanese. The jujitsu people bowed again and cleared the mat.

Somebody called out, "Aikido, line up." Most of the jujitsu people came off the mat, but some changed belts and lined up with the *aikidokas*. They went through an abbreviated version of the same ceremony. Then they formed in two lines and went through a ten-minute warmup that was

going to be hard, at least at first. It was a struggle for some
of the lower belts already on the mat.

The warm-up was a compromise between yoga and the
daily dozen of basic training, a lot of stretchers and some
push-ups and jumping jacks. Sensei led them through a series of judo falls, starting with the simplest, working into
the most complex. The last was a forward rolling breakfall,
*zenpo gaitan.* The lowest belts, the white belts, did an easy
somersault from the kneeling position, but for higher belts
the execution got more difficult, and flashier. The champ
of the forward rolling breakfall was a coldly handsome
black black-belt in Ming the Merciless beard and Klingon
samurai hairdo. He was the only *aikidoka* who wore a *hak-
ima,* the loose, flowing black pants that are the signature
of the Uishiba-style *aikidoka*, but which the Tomiki-style
reserves for extremely formal occasions. Clearly this was a
man with an attitude.

I liked him immediately, having known about a thousand
guys like that in Special Forces. His breakfall was simply
amazing. He took a short running jump, flipped over in
midair, and for a split second he *hung* upside down, perfectly vertical, with his arm extended toward the mat. Then
he dropped straight down on his arm and rolled out and up
to jog two steps and do it again.

After the falls the *aikidokas* formed up facing each other
and did kata for twenty minutes. This was the aikido I remembered, swooping circular movements designed to blend
with an attack, neutralize it, and take the opponent down.
On the street you can take those techniques one step further
and bust him up. That is not considered good form, though.
Good form is to dance your way through a situation without
hurting anybody.

After the class I was sold. I paid my first month, and
purchased my *gi* and a white belt. I was in business.

The next Thursday after work I went over and suited up
in the locker room. There were a few guys in there already,

laughing and clowning. They were nice guys; they shook hands and were friendly, but it was obviously going to take weeks before I was accepted. You have to prove yourself.

I didn't know it then, but there are a lot of casualties in aikido. Not injuries necessarily, although sometimes that too. You have to be smart; some people can't learn the moves. The thing that gets most of them is fear of flying. An awful lot of people back off from the forward rolling breakfall in the more difficult techniques. It's really scary when someone throws you into it at velocity and altitude.

After the first night I was stiff and awkward, but it was fun and I felt good going home, gym bag slung over my shoulder. Later I read in Sensei's book that Professor Tomiki, who had taught him the art, said, "As long as you do aikido you will be happy." As flat and unequivocal a statement as one could hope to find, and one for which I have no contradictory data. The higher belts in free-play, *randori*, slam each other around, something like a cross between a high-speed ballet and a demolition derby, and everybody is *grinning* at each other.

But for a white belt aikido is drill, doing the movements over and over until they become second nature, then picking up the tiny refinements that give them their power.

Over weeks of practice I began to develop an odd bond with my fellow *aikidokas*, at first with the guys I started with, and later with higher and lower belts. We were an eclectic lot; a couple of Wall Street guys, editors, both film and print, teachers, a cabbie, a court officer, an administrator, computer whizzes. When somebody transferred into aikido from other martial arts, say karate, they were on the same level with everybody else. But you could sure tell the dancers. They snapped right into the swooping, graceful movements.

When I first started aikido I wasn't thinking of the dojo as a real place. I thought of it as a place where one prepares for the street. So I went around collecting stories over coffee after class.

My karate buddies' stories are very different. Ken Kelsch, another ex-Green Beanie, a cinematographer, who's a second dan in Tae Kwon Do, if pressed, will talk about the time he was mugged by six guys, and "four of them got away."

But in aikido Matthew Winchell, who is a green belt, a midrange student, talks about the time he worked on the security squad for the Clearwater Festival. Matthew is an old hippie, a backpacker, a gentle guy, and is now an engineer for the Bureau of Ports and Trade. He said he had sneaked into the festival enough times when he was poor that he wanted to pay them back by working security. Clearwater is a folk festival, Pete Seeger, that sort of thing.

Matthew and his buddy were in the headquarters tent when the festival director told him that a big retarded kid had flipped. The boy was fifteen years old and weighed close to three hundred pounds. "He freaked out last year and it took six cops to hold him down. Think you can handle it?"

Matthew agreed to give it a try. When they arrived on the scene the boy was screaming and flailing at his mother, who was ducking and screaming back, further agitating the child. Two EMS technicians were also circling the action, looking for an opening.

When Matthew and his friend approached the senior EMS tech said, "Great! You guys are here. We'll take him down and I'll knock him out."

"Excuse me," Matthew interrupted, "but we were called in because you couldn't do this, so how does it now transpire that you are in charge?"

"Look, we're official—"

Matthew raised his hand. "Please, step back. If we can't calm him, we'll talk."

"You—"

"Please."

None too happy about it, the EMS techs retired to the edge of the crowd. Matthew approached the boy's mother, and sent her off to lunch, thus removing one irritant. By then it was obvious that attempts to restrain the boy were frustrating him, which caused him to react violently. He took a big roundhouse swing at Matthew, who lightly batted it aside, the first move in the first aikido technique, *shomen-ate*. For twenty minutes the kid took these big roundhouse swings, and for twenty minutes Matthew batted them aside. Finally the kid got tired and wound down. Matthew chatted him up for a few minutes and bought him a cotton candy. Then his mother came back and he went away happy.

My all-time favorite aikido story comes from Beverly Moon, our only woman black belt. Beverly is the mother of a grown son, an editor of books, generally in the area of comparative religion. She is not, to use Rosemary Daniell's term, *macha*. Since Beverly is completely nonthreatening I thought she might have been the target of a fair amount of harassment on the subways and on the streets.

She said, "I didn't really take aikido for self-defense. I took it for conditioning and discipline."

"Well, yeah," I insisted, "but did you ever use it in the street?"

She gave me a long ambiguous look, and shrugged. "Well, sort of," she said.

"How's that?"

"I was coming up out of the subway downtown, over on Avenue B, and there were these eight ethnic teenagers at the top of the stairs, giving me hard looks."

"Whoa! What did you do?"

"Sorted out the leader and looked him in the eye and they went away."

Sensei doesn't talk much about the philosophy of aikido. He says, "If you want to learn about *ki*, [the power that corresponds roughly to the concept of *will* in the Castaneda books] read a book. If you want to develop *ki,* practice aikido." Most of us do read the books, and were attracted to the art by its nonviolent philosophy. Trust me on this, violence gets old. But there is so much hype in the world; it's a pleasure to just *do.*

After I got integrated into the dojo it became sort of an extended family. Sometimes when Sensei was away his wife, Satomi, would take the class. This, as it turned out, was helpful. Since she's not as physically strong as Sensei she relies much more on technique. Not a difference in skill, but in emphasis. She's very good.

Sometimes when Sensei was there, but Satomi-san was busy, she'd leave her kids at the dojo. It changed the atmosphere of the place to have two Japanese cherubs, a boy and a girl, playing with block choo-choos just off the mat.

I buddied up with some more guys, mostly the people I had something else in common with; Tim Sullivan, slender and bookish editor of *Manhattan Lawyer*—quietly confident is Tim's style—and with the veterans. Manny Vargas is forty, looks thirty or younger, former Marine, former Broadway dancer, now an orthopedic nurse. Manny and I both buddied with Ray Carroll, who looks like you might imagine Ichabod Crane would look on acid. Ray's a Brit, cockney, a New York cabbie, but he used to be a demolitionist with 22 SAS in Northern Ireland, until he sort of blew himself up.

I've been shot up like Cole Younger and busted up like Evel Knievel, but Ray is a one-man orthopedic ward. Every time I got discouraged and thought perhaps I wouldn't hack it, I thought that if Ray has the balls to go out on the mat with a leg that collapses under him, then I have no excuse at all.

Members of that dojo buy a lot of Ace bandages and adhesive tape. We all have various physical deficiencies to

contend with. About six months after starting I developed
a bone spur in my right heel. At times it was difficult to
walk, much less spring off the balls of my feet into *zenpo
gaitan*. By the time I got the heel braced with a workable
combination of orthotics and elastic bandages, I had bashed
the shoulder too many times with weak launches and had
a separation of the clavicle, which is, unfortunately, a permanent condition. For several months I was in constant
low-level pain from both injuries.

What I needed was a little more muscle support for the
shoulder, so I joined a health club, but the shoulder pain
made me leery, the heel still hurt, and I had gotten scared,
so I kept bashing the shoulder with weak *zenpos*.

Then finally one day I skipped out across the mat and
dived into the air like Clark Kent making his first baby hop,
turned over, and rolled down my arm, across my back, and
out. I botched the next five, but I knew if I could do it right
once, eventually I'd be able to do it right every time.

Saturday morning, after a late Friday night. I wasn't hung
over, but I was still groggy. It had been a great night; my
wife's company had thrown its annual picnic on a cruise
ship around Manhattan, and we had juked long into the
morning after that. Plus—many pluses here—I was still
stiff from pushing too much chromed iron at the health
club. My entire upper body was sore and rigid. My right
arm is brittle from a gunshot wound in '68 that severed two
nerve trunks and one of the arteries that feed it. I know it's
brittle from having broken the hand in the past, twice, in
fits of rage, bashing doors with my fist.

So I woke up Saturday morning already crowding time
to leave, feeling, as they say back in Oklahoma, like ham-
mered shit.

But Morris's first rule of the martial arts is to show up
on time and do what you're told, and you will get better.
"Move it, fat boy," I said, and did.

I rushed in with hardly enough time to change before class, accruing more tension in my shoulders, which is where I carry it. Then the guy who led the warm-up missed all the arm and shoulder looseners.

First guy I went up with was Frederick Gear, the *zenpo* champ, giving me his best Klingon Samurai leer.

I moved in on him in the stylized attack used by new students; he grabbed my wrist and hand and slapped a *kote-gaeshi* on me. This move was totally unexpected. *Kote-gaeshi* is a reverse wrist twist. Before that I had learned it only as a counter when an opponent resists *kote-hineri*, which is the regular wrist twist. The only way to save yourself from serious damage in *kote-gaeshi,* which is a hellishly effective maneuver, is to dive over your own arm and roll out in one of those falls that I wasn't very good at.

Because I had been getting so much better Fred upped the ante and cranked on about twice the speed he had ever used on me before, which is still a long way from his top speed. And because I was so stiff and stupid I just stood there for about two beats before I started my fall. That's one and seven eights beats too long, and my right ulna, the bone in my lower right forearm, snapped like a .22 shot.

By that time I was about one third of the way through a sloppy fall, but it was still broken.

I was out five months, long enough to miss two promotion exams. Long enough to keep me in a purple belt for a year. But once or twice a month during that time I went in and watched practice, learning what I could from observation. I picked up points I might have missed otherwise. But I gave serious thought to not going back. *Kote-gaeshi* is a very common technique, and I couldn't afford a long series of broken arms. Maybe I could brace it some way.

In the absence of aikido the old poisons and discontents began to accumulate in my body. My outlook grew more sour and I found myself cursing Fred. After all, the son of a bitch had broken my arm.

But I kept on working out at home, doing the warmup as best I could, practicing the hand and foot movements. I kept working out at the health club, also as best I could. The best part was that left to its own devices, the bone spur in my right heel got better.

Eventually I suited up and went back out, still taking it easy, especially on the arm. There's really no way to brace it. The way to avoid another broken arm was to learn that scary fall. On the other hand the possibility of a broken arm is a powerful inducement to do it right.

After a few sessions I found myself loosening up. The layoff had been good for me; I was not so anxious about pushing for promotion, more ready to play for the fun I was having right now. The old loose, easy feeling was coming back, poisons burning off. I was going home with a big grin on my face again.

One night I found myself facing Fred on the mat and I thought, *I love this guy. Every time I face him I learn something and he never pushes me harder than I can handle. Uh . . . except for the time he broke my arm, and that wasn't his fault.*

I moved into my attack, aware that for once I was doing it right, not bouncing on the balls of my feet, but gliding over the mat, shoulders square, alert. He went for *kote-hineri* and I resisted. I caught just a glimpse of amusement and approval in his eyes as he shifted into a smooth, easy *kote-gaeshi* and I dived over my own arm like a dolphin at Sea World, rolling out, up, and ready to go again, a smooth, flowing, joyous move.

# The Phantom Mortar

My interview with Larry Dring for *Soldier of Fortune* re-kindled our friendship. It was the most successful story I had done for them so far. Everybody at *SOF* loved Larry. He was the heroic embodiment of everything they believed in.

A year or so later SOF sent me to Lebanon. There I fell in with some people I liked among the Lebanese Christians, and I suggested to Bob Brown, our publisher, that he send Larry over as a sort of one-man Military Training Team, which he did. Over the next two years Bob sent Larry to Lebanon three times. He taught demolitions and antitank warfare to the Christians, and learned from them as well.

In Lebanon he collected Soviet ordnance for intelligence purposes. He found small-arms innovations and weaponry that weren't in the U.S. technical manuals. The U.S. manuals said, for instance, that the Russian hand grenade had a six-second fuse. What Larry found was that they had a variable time fuse that could be set from zero to eight seconds. In war that information will save lives.

On his second trip he collected a huge bag of this stuff and took it to the intelligence officer of the Marine Amphibious Force then stationed near the airport in Beirut. This officer, a first lieutenant, had no concept of what he had, and sent it to EOD (Explosive Ordnance Demolition) to be destroyed.

On his next trip Larry painstakingly collected it all again, and brought it back, live, through customs, in a duffel bag. He figured if they checked it he'd just tell them he brought it back for the Defense Intelligence Agency, which is where Brown would send it after he'd gloated a bit in the magazine. As it happened they never opened the bag.

I was off chasing other stories by then, and was never in Lebanon with Larry. I did hear later some of the things he did. He went to outposts in the Sannine Mountains with our mutual friend Michel, who was very much like Larry, a badly damaged—in his case one-armed—super-soldier. They once captured a hash-addled Syrian GI who was convinced that they cheated when they caught him because he was invisible. They never found out why he thought that.

Even Larry was startled when Michel drove a three-quarter-ton truck over a cliff, with both of them in it. But the cliff was actually only about a seventy-five-percent grade, so they slid to the bottom in a cloud of dust.

On one occasion Larry was in a car with some Lebanese Forces people and an American woman reporter when they were ambushed by Druze gunmen. The car was turned over, and the reporter got a minor flesh wound. Larry was dinged a bit as well. Their driver got out and threw a fit. He was friends with these guys; they had ambushed the wrong car. Oh, gee, apologies all around and let's go to tea.

The week before he was to go to Lebanon for the fourth time he was hosting a backyard barbecue at his home in South Carolina when he complained of not feeling well, went inside, lay down on the sofa, and never got up. He was forty-four. Fifteen years of painkillers had weakened his heart. In truth Larry's name belongs on the Wall, as do those of a lot of guys who died of complications years later.

It wasn't until I started putting this book together that I learned my last Larry Dring story. I mentioned the project to Dale Dye. Dale is a retired Marine captain who has prospered as an actor and technical adviser in war movies. He has also written several good books, a couple of which I edited. Dale is an old friend, but I didn't know he had known Larry.

Dale met Larry in Beirut. He told me that Larry's last mission, had he returned to Lebanon, was to attempt to heal the breach between some factions of the Christian and Druze militias. He had made friends with both, and was in a position to act as honest broker.

Dale also reminded me of an event in his book *Outrage*. In the book, as in life, the Marines were forbidden to return fire without express permission from the U.S. embassy. Naturally enough when there is nothing to restrain your enemies from shooting at you they keep it up longer than they would otherwise. It is sad, but understandable, when a soldier is killed in the performance of his duty. But it is an outrage when the lives of young men are thrown away for public relations purposes, which is where Dale got the title for his book.

But somewhere out in Beirut, in Dale's book, as in life, somebody was shooting back at the bad guys in the hills. They'd fire mortars or rockets at the Marines, and before long 4.2 mortar rounds would start falling on them and they'd shut down. The Marines called it "The Phantom Mortar." The crew of the Phantom Mortar was Larry and Dale.

I've lost a lot of friends in Vietnam and in the guerrilla wars since, but none I cared more for than Larry Dring. I believe he should have won the Medal of Honor for Pleiku. He should also have been promoted to major. He wasn't promoted because, on one of his last efficiency reports, his rating officer accused him of lying. He had given Larry an order and Larry didn't do it, then denied that he had been given such an order.

No one knew then that Larry suffered some brain damage when he was wounded in Pleiku. He had lost none of his reasoning power, or his ability to learn, but he had lost some of his auditory memory. You could tell him the same joke six times and get the same laugh as the first, because he didn't remember having heard it. If he read something it was locked in forever, but he couldn't remember what he heard. That disability wasn't diagnosed until his retirement physical, long after the disastrous efficiency report.

I don't think Larry gave a damn about any of that. The Medal would have been nice, but he knew what he did. Same thing with the promotion. Of all the men I have ever known, none had a better idea of who they were than Larry, or lived life more exactly as they would have wanted to.

By rights he should have been killed at Pleiku, but he lived another fifteen years, married a great woman, had two super kids, enjoyed them all to the fullest, and died at his own party on the eve of his last crusade. Larry loved God, and I do believe God loved him back.

# Killers in Retirement

The doorway was almost hidden behind an obelisk listing the wars in which Australians had fought, and their dates. The last was Vietnam, 1962–1973, a long bloody war. I went in, followed a short hallway to another door, and found myself looking across a pool table at a darkened, noisy bar, full of middle-aged men in military haircuts.

Australian beer is the best in the world, and the national pastime seems to be knocking back fifteen or twenty of them every evening. In profile each man had a healthy gut, and what might be charitably described as a "ruddy" complexion.

At the bar I spotted the man I thought was Jack. He had a little bit of a gut, somewhat out of balance on his hipless frame, and his shoulders were set at a parade-ground angle. He looked sort of like Phil Harris, the band-leader, but his face was not ruddy; it appeared to be made of football leather. Jack Morrison: former senior regimental sergeant major of the Australian Army, most highly decorated Aussie in Korea, second award of the Distinguished Conduct Medal in Vietnam—where I had met him in the 8th Field Hospital—perhaps the bravest, and without doubt the most foul-mouthed, man I have ever met.

Still, it was dark in the bar; I had not seen him in fifteen years and had never seen him out of uniform. Just to be on the safe side I eased up to the bar. It took me a minute to get the barmaid's attention and ask, "Is that Jack Morrison?" by which time he had disappeared into the men's room.

But, at the sound of an American accent, two middle-aged men whirled and approached me. With stunning speed my hand was shaken twice and a beer slapped in it. They introduced themselves as members of Jack's company from Korea, and asked me if I had known a guy named Ray Simpson, which I had not.

Jack had been their company sergeant major in Korea and promoted both of them to sergeant. The one on the left was of Italian descent and looked sort of like the middle-aged Vic Damone. There was something oddly familiar about the other, but I couldn't place it. I didn't catch either of their names. They were both getting on a bit, and a little drunk, but there was something about their eyes. These were not shopkeepers or farmers. These were killers in genteel retirement.

"How is Jack?" I asked.

The oddly familiar one on the right did most of the talking. He wore his wavy gray hair a little long and had a handsome, intelligent face. The backs of his eyes were diamond points.

"Not so good, Jack isn't. The government's fuckin' 'im about on his disability pension, and his feet drain from the effects of Agent Orange. Has to wear special shoes." He launched on a long explanation of Jack's war with the Australian bureaucracy, which I couldn't follow very well.

Then, with no transition I can recall, he was in the middle of a war story from Korea.

"Y'know we 'ad these Korean blokes attached, not worth the powder to blow 'em to 'ell." He leaned on the bar and took a sip from his schooner. "And you know, if you 'ave to clean a grenyde, it's necessary to do it outdoors.

Anywye, this Korean sahgent's cleanin' a grenyde in the bunkah and some'ow 'e dislodges the pin and kills two of our blokes."

"And himself I suppose."

"Naow, 'e got out, and starts 'eadin' toward the CP bunkah, so I calls Jack. 'Jack,' I says. 'There's a Korean sahgent comin' your wye. Be there in a minute.'

" 'Yeh!' says Jack. 'Wot about it?'

" 'Kill 'im,' says I.

" 'Orroyt!' says Jack."

"Which," I replied, "knowing Jack, he did."

"Royt! So about foive minutes later I'm in the CP and Jack says, 'Wot was that all about?'

"So I tells 'im.

" 'Oo!' 'e says, ' 'e shouldn't a done that.' "

We laughed.

Then I felt a hand descend on my shoulder. It was Jack's. "These cunts treatin' you orroyt?" he asked.

I nodded.

"Orroyt!" he said. "Listen, I'm voice-president 'ere, and we're 'avin' a meetin'. Don't know how long it'll tyke. These girls'll tyke care of you."

"Just a minute," I said. "I have something to show you." I unzipped my overnight bag and got out a copy of my book *War Story,* in which Jack is a character. "Came twelve thousand miles to give you this."

"Royt," he said. "Give 'er a look after the meetin'." He gave his watch a quick glance, winked, and disappeared. So did the guy who looked like Vic Damone, so I was left standing at the bar with the suave, gray-haired Aussie.

"Y'know we all love Jack 'ere," he said. "But a pure warrior loike 'e is, 'e cahn't deal with a bureaucracy. We troy to protect 'im, but 'e does things 'is own wye." He described how Jack had failed to touch second base on some application for his pension. As I understood it he would come out better if he claimed a noncombat disability, and he wouldn't do it.

"Wot are you doin' 'ere?" my host asked.

"On my way to Thailand," I replied.

"Ah, Thoiland," he said. "Ever been to Singapore?"

I shook my head no. "Always wanted to."

"You know who ———— is?" He named a certain Asian head of state, sufficiently prominent to rate a couple of mentions a year in *Time*.

"Yeah, I know who he is." I wondered what mental connection he had made between my mention of Thailand and Asian politicians in Singapore.

"One toime my sahgent had 'is pistol cocked this far from 'is ear, and was about to pull the trigger." He smiled at my puzzled expression and signaled for another beer.

"My shout," I said, reaching for my pocket.

"Your money's no good 'ere," he said gruffly. "Jack said you wasn't to pye for a thing."

I shrugged and nodded thanks.

"Left seventy-foive enemy dead on that hill in Korea, Jack did. Reckon 'e'd a got the VC if he'd been a Pom." It was fairly obvious that everyone here had the same case of hero worship for Jack that I did.

My host's eyes switched back to his own story. "Y'ever 'ear of Sir ———?"

I nodded. Everybody in revolutionary warfare has heard of him, the man who fought a communist insurgency in Asia for ten years and won.

"I was a restless young bloke after Korea; couldn't find a job I liked in Australia. Answered an ad in the paper. The man said, 'Well, you've got the qualifications. Top NCO in Korea. I'll offer you a commission as lieutenant, special pay, and a paid-for vacation after every job.'"

"What was the job?"

"I was 'is bloody assassin."

Ian Fleming, that was who he reminded me of. A little

shorter and heavier, but he had the same sharp intelligent features and wiry hair.

"I have nothing against Orientals," he said, "but I hate communists. This man had been spouting the communist line and causing trouble. He was a very smart young politician, law graduate, but, we thought, a communist.

"My boss said to me, 'Ballentine, we may have to close the file on Mr. ——— ' You see, 'e always called me Ballentine, never Mr. Ballentine, never Harry. He was very British.

"The politician had about twenty-foive bodyguards there in the hotel where 'e was stayin', but they weren't difficult to get past. We went into the hotel room and I 'ad my sahgeant put 'is pistol to the man's ear. But, you see, I'd always rather buy a man than kill 'im. It's simpler in the long run. You Americans never learnt that in Vietnam."

I smiled wryly. "Of course, we could have bought them all ten times over for what we spent trying to kill them."

"Well," Harry went on, "I 'ad my sahgeant put 'is pistol to ———'s ear. 'Are you a communist?' I asked.

" 'No,' he said. 'I am not a communist.'

" 'Then why do you spout the communist line?'

" 'The communists are very popular. Don't kill me now. Perhaps we can make a deal.' Ah, 'e was a cool one. If I 'ad so much as blinked, my sahgeant would 'ave pulled the trigger. 'Come with me,' I said.

"We walked out past 'is bodyguards and I took 'im to headquarters through the back way. He was in with my boss for three hours. When 'e came out they were both smiling. 'Ballentine,' said my boss, 'I'd like you to meet the next president of ———.' And we shook 'ands all round."

"He's still in power," I said.

"Yes, and the British are still secretly in control. As I said, it's easier to buy them.

" 'Will I see you again, Mr. Ballentine?' the politician asked. At that my boss looked startled. 'If you see Mr.

Ballentine again,' 'e said, 'he will be the last person you ever see!' "

"Have you ever seen him again?" I asked.

"Oh, no," Harry replied. "I would never go to 'is country. "E might think I was still active and take preventive measures.

"That sahgeant of mine was an interesting specimen," he went on. "When I took the job I had a thirty-six-man platoon, all 'and-picked men, but no sergeant. My boss suggested I interview this chap at the jail awaiting execution. He was a Choinese tong killah. I went down there. 'Look,' I said, 'I can 'ave you out of 'ere this afternoon. You come to work for me. I'll make you a sergeant. You get special pay, and a paid-for-leave after each job. And after two years, a pardon.' He thought about it for a long time. 'Well,' he said, 'it's better than doyin'." He laughed. " 'Better than doyin',' " he repeated.

He started to signal for another beer. "Listen," I said. "I haven't eaten since noon, and I'm not used to this stuff. If I don't get something in my stomach soon you're going to have a sloppy-drunk on your hands."

"Fish and chips orroyt or do you want a hamburger?"

I smiled. "Fish and chips is fine."

It was fully dark and the air crisp as we walked through the streets of that run-down commercial area of Melbourne. It was July, early winter in Australia. I had a bit of a buzz on, and wondered why he was telling me all this. One of the reasons I had come to Melbourne was to see if Jack would be interested in an interview on his wartime experiences; and now here was this other story. It was good, and had an authentic ring to it, but on the other hand you run into a lot of bullshit artists. Anyway, I enjoyed the conversation.

We went down a block and over two, crossing the railroad tracks, and went into what is called a "take-away" in Australia—a carryout place. Harry had fish and chips and

I had a chiko roll, which resembles an oversize eggroll—and holds roughly the same position in Australian society that a taco does in the American Southwest. We squeezed into a back booth at the take-away and I smiled at the thought of Ian Fleming and James Bond's gourmet meals. "You mind if I use some of this stuff?" I asked, meaning his experiences.

He looked at me closely, to see if I was the kind of journalist who would betray a confidence. "Don't use ————'s real name." he said. "That would be very embarrassing."

"Don't worry, I won't." I had no desire to hurt an ally who ran what appeared to be a relatively prosperous and happy country. "What about your name?"

He pondered for a minute. "Call me . . . Wong!" he grinned and uttered a short barking laugh. I didn't do that, but his name is not exactly Ballentine either.

"If you write this," he said around a mouthful of chips, "there's a story you should use.

"There was a Choinese lady in our unit who operated alone, a lovely thing she was; always carried a .32 in 'er bra. The communists killed her 'usband and she had joined our unit for revenge. Ah, Gawd! She was beautiful and I wanted her; tried everything I knew to get her and nothing worked.

"One evening, shortly after I had received a new assignment, she appeared at my bungalow. 'The man you have just been assigned to kill is the man who murdered my husband. I want him.'

" 'I couldn't do that,' I replied. 'This is a professional job, not a vendetta.'

" 'You will get two weeks' leave after the job,' she said. 'I will spend those two weeks with you, and I guarantee you will remember them always as the best two weeks of your life!' "

I had been skeptical before, and that sounded way too perfect. But when he smiled at the memory—a slow, disingenuous, reminiscent smirk—it was not the smile of a man running a con.

"My platoon had him surrounded in an alley; he came out the door. We caught him full in the searchlight. I promised Florence the first three shots, and they were two more than she needed."

"How was your vacation?"

"Best one I ever 'ad," he replied. "But when I got back the boss called me in. 'When two of my best agents go to the same place at the same time I become curious,' he said. 'You're good, but she's better than you. I don't want her effectiveness impaired in any way.' So I told him what had happened."

"Was he pissed?"

"No. 'E didn't care as long as it wasn't permanent. He didn't want 'er married."

"Did you take her out after that?"

"No." There was a touch of wistfulness in his reply. I believed him then.

"You must have had some strange romantic encounters in a position like that."

"I had a maid I was very fond of. Been sleepin' with 'er for two years. She asked for toime off to visit 'er sick mother. I don't know what she was thinkin' of, because I'd checked 'er out thoroughly, and knew 'er mother was dead.

"So I let her go and stayed up that noight. When the first knock came I put a six-round burst from a Sten through the door. They left royt awye and there were three blood trails into the bush outside my door. They never bothered me at home after that.

"I worried a bit about what to do to her. She set me up, but I'm sure she was under a death threat at the toime. I 'ad to do something, though, or appear soft. So I fixed her up with a couple of years' easy detention. Not too bad.

"One other toime there was a Malay actress I wanted badly. Tried everything. Sent 'er flowers; sent 'er candy.

Nothing. Then I got a message to meet her in a certain restaurant. Should'ave known then, but I went.

"An 'alf hour after she was supposed to arroive, the hair on the back of me neck stood up, which has saved me more than once. Two Choinese men who looked familiar came in the restaurant, but I already 'ad my pistol under the table. When the first one got 'is out, I hit 'im first. But the second one grabbed 'im and held 'im in front, and started foirin'. I 'ad to 'it 'im in the 'ead, and by that toime I 'ad a wound in me gut. Got 'im, though."

I took a bite out of the chiko roll.

Much refreshed from having lined our stomachs with grease, we once again stepped into the nippy air between the take-away and the Returned Servicemen's League.

When we entered its dark, boozy interior, I spotted Jack over by the bar with my AWOL bag, bent over my book in the dim light. It was open to the part, about two thirds of the way through, where he makes his appearance.

He sat next to a dark-haired lady of almost his age, who looked about how one might expect Raquel Welch to look in fifteen years, if her luck holds. Jack looked up like a kid caught with his hand in the cookie jar, and quickly shoved the book back into the AWOL bag. Harry introduced me to Jack's wife, Pat, and while that was happening Jack disappeared again.

My ears are all blown out from a combination of artillery, aircraft engines, and heavy-metal rock 'n' roll, so I could scarcely understand what was said, but somehow she got the idea from Harry that either I hadn't eaten, or hadn't eaten enough. She reached into her purse and pulled out a slice of baklava wrapped in waxed paper, and offered it to me with a touchingly tender smile, such as I have never seen on Raquel Welch.

There was a schooner of Victoria bitter in my left hand, and a slice of sweet Greek pastry in my right. I was at a loss as to how to proceed.

Harry was in my ear with another story. "Shot this bloke dead in the street, and I 'ad nothing to prove who 'e was, so, much to my surprise, I was arrested. 'This toime, Mr. Ballentine, you've gone too far,' says the inspector.

" 'Don't let it come to troial, man,' I told him. 'You don't know who you're dealin' with.'

" 'I am a professional police officer,' 'e says. 'I do moy job accordin' to the law.'

" 'Don't ruin yourself, man,' I told him. 'This isn't London. We aren't foightin' criminals; we're foightin' bloody communist insurgents, and none of the rules apply.' "

"So what happened?" I asked. I made short work of the baklava and licked my fingers.

"They flew a magistrate out from London for the troial. I was acquitted, and the inspector was sent 'ome, shakin' 'is 'ead. 'I cahn't understand it,' 'e said. 'I've been a dedicated policeman for thirty years.'

" 'Told you this was war, man,' I told him. 'You can't interfere with the secret police.' "

I heard a loud electronic click and Jack's voice boomed over the PA system, rumbling like gravel in a steel chute. "Me mate Jimmy Morris . . . came all the wye from America to see me . . . moy shout . . . step to the bar." A moment later he was back at the bar, smiling, charged with energy.

Soon I met a whole procession of Aussies—the old and grizzled, and the young, T-shirted, and bearded. They were all slightly drunk and they all had the look of combat men, with enlarged facial pores, and smiles that knew too much. But there was a genuine openness there. I liked all of them and they accepted me as one of their own. I understood them much better than I understand American civilians. Combat is one of those experiences that unite all who have had it. I would be far more at home at a gathering of ex-VC and NVA than I would be at a meeting of the junior chamber of commerce in my own hometown.

Suddenly the PA clicked on again and a voice said, "Noine o'clock." Everyone in the room stood up and all the lights went out except for one small spot that illuminated something hung on the left wall, which I couldn't make out. I had forgotten. This was the Nine O'clock Silence, a nightly memoriam to Australian servicemen killed in war. I had been told about it by an Aussie lady: "Sort of pathetic, really, all these drunken old sods, living in the past." But I did not find it so. Normally my reactions to ceremonies of this sort range from indifference to cynicism, but this night I was touched by the obvious sincerity of these people's feelings. The voice on the PA recited:

> *"In Flanders fields the poppies blow*
> *Between the crosses, row on row,*
> *That mark our place; and in the sky*
> *The larks, still bravely singing, fly,*
> *Scarce heard amid the guns below.*
>
> *We are the dead. Short days ago*
> *We lived, felt dawn, saw sunset glow,*
> *Loved and were loved, and now we lie*
> *In Flanders Fields.*
>
> *Take up our quarrel with the foe.*
> *To you from failing hands we throw*
> *The torch; be yours to hold it high.*
> *If you break faith with us who die,*
> *We shall not sleep, though poppies grow*
> *In Flanders Fields."**

And in response everyone there but I, who did not know the ceremony, responded in chorus:

---

*Colonel John McRae, who died in France through illness contracted during WWI. His poem is published by courtesy of the proprietors of *Punch*, owners of the copyright.

> *"We shall not forget them.*
> *We shall not forget them.*
> *We shall not forget them."*

The lights came back up, the noise level rose, and I buried my nose in the foam.

"Ah, 'tis a beautiful thing!" Jack said.

Shortly after that I found myself in a car with Harry, Pat, and Jack. Harry was driving.

It seemed a fairly short trip to Jack's house and I suppose there was conversation, although I don't remember any of it, except for one comment of Harry's about me. " 'E doesn't miss much; I was watchin' 'is eyes at the club." It is true that I don't miss much, but I hadn't caught Harry watching my eyes, so I must presume he misses less than I do.

Jack's house is over a hundred years old, and he proudly showed me through, showing off the workmanship on the old fireplaces. Then he placed my book on the shelf with his other books on war. Over the fireplace was a copy of a painting of a younger Sergeant Major Jack Morrison, the hero of Korea. He was thinner in it, and seemed more grim than the man I knew.

"It's a copy of one in the army museum in Canberra," Harry said. "The government paid ten thousand for it."

Jack, standing there, swelled visibly with pride. He unabashedly gloried in being a legend in his own time, although I have never heard him brag, and was unable to extract the story from him I thought I had come for.

After that Jack took me outside to show me two Peking ducks he had penned up in the backyard. We shared a whiz on the grass and went inside for another beer.

Pat and Harry had cracked two bottles of Victoria bitter and we went into the living room where the record player was. For my edification Jack played a record of the English tenor Peter Dawson, singing an album of military songs, notably the "Ballad of Private Roger Young" and "The Sergeant Major on Parade." I enjoyed Jack's enthusiasm as he raised his glass, pumping his right arm in time to the music, and sang along. Pat gazed at Jack in what looked to me like plain, flat-out adoration. Harry looked at them both fondly.

"Pat's not Australian," he said. "She's cockney, Jack met her in London. I love 'er, you know. But don't tell Jack. 'E'd kill me. I gave him me own pistol; seventeen personal kills on it, and 'e'd do the eighteenth, and it'd be me."

During a break between songs Pat held Jack's arm and asked, "Are y'doin' orroyt, beloved?"

He gazed at her with the most tender, loving look I have ever seen a man give a woman, smiled wryly, and said, "Oi'm doin' foine, y'poisonous Pommy bahstid."

After the military songs Pat put on a Dean Martin album and she and Jack danced, quite well, and Harry told me another story. "There was a man, a very dangerous man, and no one had been able to remove him. I was asked if I could do the job. I said yes."

"How?" I asked. We stood by the fireplace, with our glasses of Victoria bitter. I was not incapacitated, but I had drunk more than I wanted. My belly was tight. Harry was still sipping along at about the same rate he had all evening.

"I got to him through his brother. First I arranged for his business to make about four hundred pounds a month more than it had, for four months. Then I cut him off. By then he'd bought a new house and a new car; gained a whole new level of expectations. After the second month he was desperate. That's when I approached him. I convinced him that I didn't want his brother's life. I told him that his brother would be in jail for two years and that, after that, I'd set him up with a new identity and a new location. In the meantime I'd get him out of debt, and see he 'ad some left over."

"Was that what you wanted?"

"No, I killed his brother. When my informant found out what he'd done he committed suicide. What the 'ell! I slept that noight. It's a rough game."

This time I was watching Harry's eyes. Somewhere back down in there he flinched. He may have slept well the night it happened, but I'll wager he's lost some sleep over the years since. I was beginning to understand his reason for telling me these stories.

The dance ended and Jack and Pat joined us. Jack asked Pat to get an album of clips and pictures of his military career. There were stories about his DCM and Bar, about his retirement, with pictures of him in garrison cap and Sam Browne belt. He looked ill at ease in them. Jack was a field soldier, pure and simple.

Among the pictures was one of him when he first joined the service in World War II, as merry a lad as you'd ever want to see, with guileless eyes and a reckless grin, his slouch hat worn at the same nonregulation, if not impossible, angle he'd worn it at in the hospital.

"Just a young trooper," he said, and laughed. What I saw was a classic example of the kind of kid who drives his sergeant to drink or insanity.

He also proudly showed me a picture of his daughter, married to a younger retired regimental sergeant major, now doing well as a painting contractor. "She made a foine army woife, with her upbringin'," he said.

Jack and Pat danced the next dance, and I talked to Harry again. This time we leaned against a wall on the opposite side of the room. He leaned forward, speaking softly and earnestly. This time there was no pretense. Here was a man baring his soul.

"We attacked a terrorist camp, and took a woman prisoner. She must have been high up in the party. She wore the red tabs of a commissar. I'd already told my men we took no prisoners, but I'd never killed a woman. 'She must die quickly; we must leave!' my sergeant said.

"Oh, God, I was sweatin'," Harry went on. "She was magnificent. 'What's the matter, Mr. Ballentine?' she asked. 'You're sweatin'.'

" 'Not for you'," I said. " 'It's a malaria recurrence.' I gave my pistol to my sergeant, but he just shook his head. I had got this man out of prison. None of them would do it. None of them would do it, and if I didn't I'd never be able to control that unit again.

" 'You're sweatin', Mr. Ballentine,' she said again.

" 'Not for you,' I said.

"Did you kill her?"

"Hell, I blew 'er fuckin' 'ead off," he replied.

Jack and Pat glided by to the waning notes of *"Volare."*

"My platoon all gathered round and smiled. 'You are our *tuan*,' my sergeant said. 'You are our *tuan*.' "

I'm not a priest; I'm not even an officer anymore. I had never let my Montagnards kill prisoners. But I'd quit interrogating them because I was starting to like it. That was not something I had wanted to know about myself. And we've all seen good men die because we weren't exactly in top form that particular day. I had forgiven myself for that. I hoped my look told Harry that I liked him, that it was okay with me if he forgave himself. It's hard to do, though. The only way you can accept that you're not a villain is to admit you're not a hero either.

The record ended. We had another beer. Harry went home and after a while we all went to bed.

Pat had already gone to work when I got up the following morning. Jack was in the kitchen frying both of us a steak for breakfast.

There was something that had been bothering me. I try to be as honest as I can in my writing, and sometimes I worry that things I say about my friends might hit them the wrong way. "Let me read you what I wrote about you," I said to Jack.

"I read it, myte," he said, over the skillet.

"I hope you weren't offended when I called you a 'beat-up old duffer.' "

He smiled a little wryly. "I wasn't offended, myte."

After breakfast we got in Jack's car. I still hadn't got used to the driver's side being on the right, and more than once I had been almost creamed by an oncoming car, stepping off the curb looking the wrong way.

"This part of Melbourne's all Greek," Jack said. "Melbourne's got the third largest Greek population of any city in the world."

Jack had suggested, with no dissent on my part, that he show me some of the Australian paintings in the National Museum, where he worked as a guards officer. The streets changed into broad parklike boulevards as we neared the museum. There was just the suggestion of a nip, and no flowers bloomed, but the palm trees grew along the boulevard; it was a British city in the tropics.

"I helped build this street when I was a young fella," Jack said.

The museum was a beautiful modern structure, with a banner outside advertising a Pompeii exhibit I had seen in Dallas a year or so previously.

Inside, I checked my AWOL bag and Jack explained to the guard on duty what he was doing. "The guards are all retired warrant officers," Jack explained. A warrant officer in the Australian army is what we would call a senior NCO in ours. I grinned inside, thinking of those old sergeants major, working in that museum after decades of army life. I fancied I could detect a mellowing effect.

Jack had a pretty clear idea of what he wanted to show me, and I had to drag my feet to pause by some brilliantly designed glass sculptures, flashing translucent primary colors. He blasted right through the modern and impressionist section, and barged back to the seventeenth- and eighteenth-century stuff, to show me some dark and brooding English landscapes. His only judgment was "There's not an 'ell of a lot of difference between a Turner and a Constable."

When we had seen what he wanted to show me, I insisted on going back to the moderns, and to the Impressionists, which are my favorites. Jack stood off to the side and pretended not to know me while I examined some of them closely. But the comments he did make, particularly about the porcelain and the Australian painting, showed he hadn't been sleepwalking during his time in the museum.

"Did you have any interest in this stuff before you came to work here?" I asked.

"No," he replied.

We left the museum and turned left toward the business district. Jack told me that the park across the street was the home of ducks that sometimes decide to cross with their ducklings, and that the cops would leap out and stop traffic for them.

We walked across the bridge and over the River Yarra, which reminded me somewhat of pictures I've seen of the Seine in Paris. It's not very much like that, but it is more like that than either the North Canadian where it runs through Oklahoma City, or the Mekong in Phnom Penh, the rivers through cities that I knew.

A block past the railway station Jack turned into a pub. Inwardly I cringed. It was only ten-thirty in the morning and I am not much of a drinker. I had probably drunk more beer in the past two weeks in Australia than in the preceding decade. But it was an hour and a half until my ride left for Wagga Wagga, and I was enjoying Jack's company.

"Nothing I loike better'n a pot o' beer," Jack said as we stepped up to the bar, all dark wood and tasteful appointments.

"See that paintin'." Jack pointed out a huge floor-to-ceiling nude in an elaborate gold frame, extremely well done, of a gorgeous young girl of surpassing innocence.

"That's Chloe," he said. "That's a very famous paintin'.

The whole city of Melbourne's proud of 'er. During the war some of your blokes, Marines they were, tried to steal her. Six of 'em, drunk, some'ow got 'er out of the frame; 'ad 'er rolled up and ready to go out the door. They gave 'er back without a foight when it was explyned 'ow important she was."

A voice broke in over Jack's shoulder. "Cracky Jack Morrison, from Korea, by God." The speaker was in bad shape. It was ten-thirty in the morning and he was shitfaced. He was clean shaven and well dressed in a tweed leisure suit. But he had the face and slurred speech of an old wino.

"Hello, cobber," Jack said.

Sure enough, this man had been in Jack's company in Korea. He launched on a long, disjointed remembrance of experiences they had shared, and explained that his daughter and son-in-law were keeping him now. They had celebrated his birthday the previous evening, and kept his glass full all night.

"This is me myte, Jimmy Morris," Jack said. "We were drinkin' with Killer Ballentine just last noight." We shook hands. It was like grabbing a sponge full of dishwater.

"Killer, eh?" And this sparked another round of war stories.

I didn't want to knock Jack's friend, but when he left I said, "He doesn't seem to be right on top of it."

"Aghh!" said Jack. " 'E's gone! Shouldn't even be aloive. Most of 'is stomach's missin'." Then Jack did something I had seen him do three or four times in the last couple of days. He raised his glass and stopped halfway to his lips. Stopped dead, rigid, as though he had stepped out of time, and his eyes were somewhere else. It was not a thousand-yard stare, but as though he were sharing a toast with a whole lot of people I couldn't see. At such times he had the mouth of a child, but his eyes were the oldest things I have ever seen. It only lasted a second, and then he meditatively sipped his beer.

"We alwyes called 'im Killer," he said. "He was in a special unit for seven years, you know."

"He mentioned that."

Jack smiled a little. " 'E's in love with me woife."

I nodded. "He told me that, too, but he said he couldn't tell you, because you'd kill him."

Jack smiled. " 'E's a good lad, Killer is. There's no 'arm in 'im. 'E's all shot full o' holes now, though."

For the first time I noticed Jack's right arm was much thinner than the left. "What happened to your arm?"

"Ah, took a round in me neck. Affected the nerves."

My own right arm is somewhat withered, missing a couple of nerves and an artery from gunshot wounds, something else we had in common.

"Bad feet, bad arm, the lot," Jack said. "But I'd do it all again."

"Yeah," I admitted, somewhat ruefully. "Me too."

Things are much simpler where you don't know the people you hurt.

"Did you know Ray Simpson in the 8th Field, Jim?"

I shook my head.

"Black Australian warrant officer. 'Is woife was Japanese, and the government denoied 'er pension because she 'adn't been an Australian resident for foive years. Two kids. 'E 'ad the Victoria Cross, the lot. The RSL finally got a special bill passed givin' 'er a pension of two 'undred a month. Wot'll that buy in Tokyo todye, Jim? Coupla fish 'eads and roice. We're still workin' on gettin' 'er the full pension. We'll get it for 'er."

Soon it was time for him to go. We went to the door and shook hands. I watched him go to the stoplight. He never looked back, only waited for the light to change, and stepped off the curb with his left foot, taking thirty-inch steps, 120 to the minute.